SECRETS OF
SUCCESSFUL
SALES

ALISON EDGAR

The Entrepreneur's Godmother

Secrets of Successful Sales

First published in 2018 by

Panoma Press Ltd
48 St Vincent Drive, St Albans, Herts, AL1 5SJ, UK
info@panomapress.com
www.panomapress.com

Book layout by Neil Coe.

Printed on acid-free paper from managed forests.

ISBN 978-1-784521-29-5

A CIP catalogue record for this book is available from the British Library.

This book is available online and in bookstores.

TESTIMONIALS

"Alison's sales methodology works and makes selling easy and fun! This book is a must have for anyone who wants to master the art of selling."

Ben Towers, Award-winning Entrepreneur, named by The Times at the top of the world's Super Teen Power List

"A simple and effective approach to sales, this is a must read for anyone who wants to start and grow a successful business."

Warren Cass, Speaker, Entrepreneur and Best Selling Author of *Influence*

"Alison Edgar is one of the most entrepreneurial people that we have ever come across at Enterprise Nation. Alison inspires people to start a business and then applies her skills to help them grow. The entrepreneurial landscape in Britain is a better place with her in it."

Emma Jones MBE, Founder of Enterprise Nation, and Small Business Representative to the Crown

"Alison Edgar is rightly considered to be an expert in her field. With a wealth of experience and the ability to utilise a range of methodologies, Alison has a proven track record of not only helping entrepreneurs, but also supporting and guiding seasoned sales professionals to achieve even greater success. This is a must read for anyone working in the sales profession – not to be missed."

Thomas Moverley, Corporate Account Director, The Institute of Sales Management

ACKNOWLEDGEMENTS

Being dyslexic I always felt writing a book was something I couldn't do. I would like to thank Natasha Baer and Gemma Philpott for welcoming me to the world of words, and reminding me I can do anything if I put my mind to it.

As always, a huge heartfelt thank you to Loraine Lester for giving me the push to set up my own business. And hugs and kisses to Ross Butler for naming me 'The Entrepreneur's Godmother' – it seems to have stuck.

None of this would have been possible without the help and support of my ever-patient husband Neil and amazing sons Kieran and Connor. I would not have been able to achieve the things I have without you, but hold on to your hats, I'm only getting started!

I surround myself with entrepreneurs who inspire me every day, especially my young pack, Ben Towers, Simon Crowther and Jordan Daykin. Keep being fabulous.

Thanks to Mindy Gibbins-Klein and her team at Panoma Press and to Marc Leverton for his work in the initial stages of the book.

There is one person who deserves an extra special mention because without her help this book would not have been possible. She has taken my methodology, my voice, and my written work, and turned it into a book. For this, I will be forever grateful, not just for me but for all the readers who will be able to transform their sales and futures. Kiya Newnham, the words 'Thank You' do not seem even nearly adequate enough, but they are all I have.

FOREWORD

By Emma Jones MBE, Founder of Enterprise Nation and Small Business Representative to the Crown

As an American entrepreneur once said to me, "If you're not making sales, you don't have a business" and it's as true today as it was a decade ago when this was uttered. As a founder and business owner, you're always pitching, and sales are that vital end result to keep money flowing, employees in work, and the balance sheet strong.

There's no better person to teach these skills than Alison Edgar. In this book she delves into how you can make sales through understanding behaviour (yours and others), and keep the sales coming in by building strong relationships. The advice is not just theory – it's based on practical experience – and is well worth following.

I highly recommend this book to all aspiring entrepreneurs and anyone who wants to excel in sales.

CONTENTS

INTRODUCTION

Hi, I'm Alison Edgar – The Entrepreneur's Godmother.

'Godmother' – a woman who is influential or pioneering in a movement or organisation.

Yip, I agree it is a quirky name, but it's what one of my clients called me and it stuck. Before I introduce myself formally, I think now is a good time to answer a question which I would be asking if I were in your shoes.

There are hundreds of books on sales and even more sales trainers and coaches, so what makes me different? Good question. Let me explain. It is by taking what I learned working in the corporate sales arena for over 25 years, and combining it with modern methods, which has allowed me to come up with something unique.

I am sure we have all had to deal with salespeople at one stage or another in our life. Some we have bought from, some we have not. Salespeople are an unusual breed, and without tarring them all with the same brush... many think they are the best thing since sliced bread (as my grannie used to say)!

It was at an annual sales conference in Reading that the idea for my methodology was born. Wow, the amount of hot air being generated by 250 salespeople in the room was enough to float the Madejski Stadium to the moon. I overheard snippets of conversations everywhere about how fantastic they all were and how they were 'smashing targets', 'winning this', 'earning that'. But the truth was, some were and some weren't. This event opened my eyes to different types of sales performers:

The Firework – like a rocket when they start a sales role they reach the sky, but after one hit they fizzle out and disappear.

The Steady Eddie – tending to be with companies a long time, they will usually be around the target line, just happy to plod along, never going to set the world alight.

The Wrong Job – the draw of sales and the fine things that come with it is not quite as glamorous as it looks when it's wrapped up with hard knocks and rejection. Sales, like entrepreneurism, is not for everyone.

The Fantasist – these are the ones who forecast amazing things but can't close the deals. Their words speak louder than their actions.

The Desperate – people say and do things out of character when they are under pressure. Unfortunately, this sometimes leads to them not telling the truth which is why historically sales sometimes get a bad name and can be thought of as pushy.

The Complainer – it is never their fault they don't hit target, it is the company's, the customer's, the manager's. Everyone else is to blame but them.

Then there are THE STARS, the ones who:

S – Stay positive

T – Tenacious

A – Always focused

R – Resilient

S – Successful

Not only do they consistently hit their target but always overachieve. As soon as there is an incentive they create a strategy to win. They can work with the same company for years as they build strong relationships and bond trust with their customers which means their competitors can't even get a foot in the door. They are confident without being cocky, they are assertive without being aggressive and they can read situations and adapt. They are the ones the other types of salespeople knock as being 'lucky' because they can't see the early mornings and the late finishes and the additional things the STARS do to make the customer experience unforgettable. They can tell you to the penny where they are to target at any time and how much commission they are going to make because they are laser focused on their goals and have the tenacity to achieve them. They look at their role as running their own businesses and the product or service they sell is just the vehicle of the brand to allow them to be in charge of their own destiny. They are always positive and adapt well to change, finding a new way to do things even when the goalposts are moved. Bad days happen but they are quick to bounce back and concentrate on the good days.

Which one was I? Of course, I was and always will be one of the STARS, but you don't have to take my word, check out my LinkedIn account and read the reviews from my customers, managers and peers. Make sure you learn habits from someone who has done it and done it well. Anyone can write a book, so do your research. Would you rather take football tips from David Beckham or Dave Smith from the Dog and Duck Sunday League football team?

I created my methodology from studying what I do and other top performers do to become the STARS. My teaching does not come from regurgitating other people's textbook content, it comes from real life experiences and gives you everything you need to be able to sell.

Ok, so I hope by now you will realise I know my stuff when it comes to sales, but what about business and entrepreneurship?

In just 18 months after incorporating my company, I quadrupled my turnover to six figures, tripled my workforce, was voted one of the UK's top ten business advisers, becoming an award-winning Great British Entrepreneur, and was shortlisted for a lifetime achievement award by the Institute of Sales and Marketing Management. I have been featured in *The Sunday Times*, *The Telegraph*, *The Guardian*, *The*

Mail on Sunday, BBC radio, as well as being invited for afternoon tea by the Queen.

In 2015 the government closed down all match funding services that enabled small businesses to access specialist training. As a small business owner, I knew how hard it could be, and knew that the withdrawal of match funding meant it was about to get a whole lot harder. That's when I waved my wand and became The Entrepreneur's Godmother. I created a whole new brand devoted to startups, micros, and owner-managed businesses, helping them access specialist sales training at an affordable and accessible rate. In one year since rebranding, I have developed online products, taken my business international and been a feature on BBC Breakfast for three consecutive weeks to share my views and opinions around the small business community. Before May 2016 no one even knew who or what The Entrepreneur's Godmother was, and now you're reading my book.

Some people think what I have done is remarkable; I believe that you can achieve anything you put your mind to. So, well done you! You have taken the first step to becoming a sales hero. Now it's in your hands to put what you will learn into your business and fly.

Who is this book for?

- Firstly, everyone!

  Everything we do in business is built on a sale. This book will give you the inspiration and confidence to believe in yourself and your abilities, especially if you currently HATE sales.

- Secondly, entrepreneurs starting a business. No sales = no business. It is that simple.

- Thirdly, people working in sales (and marketing). I have testimonials from people who have worked in sales for over 30 years who have learned new things from working with me.

- Fourthly, intrepreneurs. Intrepreneurship is rapidly building in lots of companies in the world. This is the idea that employees working in larger corporates take more of an entrepreneurial attitude towards their role.

- Finally, people who have a business and are looking to upscale and need help with growing their team.

Everyone is a salesperson, whether it is getting someone to make you a cup of tea or closing a million-pound deal, the secret is reaching the win-win situation. Of course, in business, we couldn't thrive if people paid us in cups of tea, but it is not only about closing sales, it is also about getting the right margins.

Anyone can sell at a bargain price, but the secret of being an entrepreneur is making money.

My Glamorous Golfing Career

At age 11 I was introduced to golf, the main reason being my Mum and Dad were members of Clydebank and District Golf Club. My parents, Alistair and Jessie, both really enjoyed it and it was not unusual for them to play two or three times a week, sometimes more in the summer months. Being too young to be left home alone, I was frequently promoted to 'caddy' on our outings to the golf club. But this quickly wore thin when the stash of crisps and fizzy pop ran out.

After many tantrums and false threats of 'running away to join the circus', it became apparent that in order to make my pre-teens bearable, things had to change. So, I opted for the 'if you can't beat them join them' motto.

My parents were chuffed I had come around to their way of thinking, and with a tatty old bag and a mismatch of clubs (second hand would be an understatement, maybe 10th or 11th hand would be more accurate) I decided to take up golf. Hey, how hard could it be? I'd seen people play and 'caddied' often enough and surely I would be a natural at it.

That couldn't have been further from the truth. I HATED it. I am surprised there was a golf course left for the other players the way I would hack up the fairway, not to mention the numerous fresh air shots, and cries from my Mum of 'You are lifting your head'.

Grrrrrrr. So, what were my options? I was still too young to be 'home alone' (who knows, I may have become the Clydebank version of Macaulay Culkin). As whinging and moaning was falling on deaf ears, it was up to me to move across the line from hate to love. To do that I had to move from bad at golf to good. To do this I decided to remove myself from the course, which I am sure the other golfers were relieved about as it meant their balls weren't landing in my moon crater-sized indentations.

After a series of intense professional lessons, I learned the core skills I needed to play – an interlock grip, a good open stance and fluid swing. I decided to set up camp on the practice fairway because here it didn't matter how good you were, there were no impatient players to hold up. I became like a boomerang: hit the balls, fetch the balls, repeat. Hour after hour just doing the same thing, with my driver, five iron and pitching wedge. Then, as if by magic, a great thing happened. The fresh air shots and massive hacks of grass became less and less, something was changing. I was getting better, and I actually started to quite like golf!

Over the years my abilities grew and my handicap reduced. By the age of 16 I was playing with a handicap of 12 (for those who know nothing about golf, the maximum handicap for ladies at that time was 36 at the beginner level and 0 at the professional level). I had been taken under the wing of Jock, an ex-professional player who gave his time to coach and mentor me, analysing my grip and swing until I had perfected my own methods. I even had the honour of being chosen for the club, county and West of Scotland teams. I actually

LOVED golf and spent as many hours as possible playing, sometimes doing two rounds in one day.

So how can you take my golf analogy and apply it to sales?

1. You have to want to, because if you don't want to, you never will. You have a choice – to whine and moan or to do something about it.

2. Take specialist advice at the start of your journey, get professional help to teach you. Otherwise, you will start with self-taught bad habits, and will never reach your peak.

3. Learn sales methodology and techniques. I genuinely believe when it's delivered correctly *sales and customer service* are EXACTLY the same thing. I teach my four key pillar areas of sales: behaviours, sales process, sales strategy and confidence. This gives a firm structure and teaches you the rules of sales.

4. Practice, practice, practice and practice again. Human nature teaches us we love things we are good at, and the only way to get good is doing things over and over again. You don't become a professional at anything without practising every day.

5. Embrace the rejections, don't fear them. In the words of my buddy, Will King, the CEO of King of Shaves, *"A no is not forever, just for now"*. Sales is a numbers game, and for every no, you are one step closer to a yes.

6. Mindset, if you don't believe you can sell you won't be able to sell. Have *confidence* in your products and services; if you don't your customers won't buy. If you need to make improvements to what you do, go and do it, then come back with gusto ready to hit the market.

7. Don't ignore the problem; hating it will not make it go away. Sales are the lifeblood of any business. If you don't sell you don't have a business. Poor sales and cash flow are the main reasons businesses fail. Take action before it's too late.

8. Always look for new ways. Marketing is evolving every day. *Use social media and marketing to raise your brand awareness* to help generate enquiries from people who are aware of your company – this makes converting them to customers easier.

Embrace it, enjoy it. Closing a sale is an adrenaline rush and everyone needs that in their life.

Developing Your Mindset

To be one of the STARS in sales you have to stay positive and be resilient. As an entrepreneur or salesperson, you will get a lot of knock-backs, people telling you 'No' and failing to see the beauty in your business idea. So how do you do this? How do you take the rejection and turn it into something positive? Well, it's all about having a growth mindset. This theory is a fairly new discovery for me but something that has become extremely relevant and important in my life. That's why I want to share with you my journey on the way to a growth mindset.

Recently I was flicking through my Facebook feed when something on a post really grabbed my attention. One of my friends had posted she was sick of the negative comments which were coming up on threads, and it was someone's reply that pricked my interest. A comment on the post said to be more forgiving as the negativity was coming from people with a fixed mindset.

I had heard of fixed and growth mindsets, but didn't know much about them. Researching the topic, I have been through an emotional, heart-wrenching journey which I want to share with you.

Carol Dweck, Professor of Psychology at Stanford University, is the leading expert in the field of Mindset. What I have written here is based on her research, not something I made up in the car on the way to work. The table below shows some typical traits of growth and fixed mindset.

Growth Mindset	Fixed Mindset
I can learn anything I want to	I'm either good at it, or I'm not
When I'm frustrated, I persevere	When I'm frustrated, I give up
I want to challenge myself	I don't like to be challenged
When I fail, I learn	When I fail, I'm no good
Tell me I try hard	Tell me I'm smart
If you succeed, I'm Inspired	If you succeed, I feel threatened
My effort and attitude determine everything	My abilities determine everything

It got me to thinking about how a mindset is formed? Is it nature or nurture? Can you change from fixed to growth and vice versa? It was during this thought-provoking time and while I was looking for a story that people would relate to, I realised I had an example which was very close to home.

In 1943 in the middle of World War II, my father, Alistair, then aged eight, had been knocked down by a bike, leaving him with injuries which left him unable to walk properly for the rest of his life. His injuries meant he had to stay in hospital for a long time, with a knock-on effect of missing school. The education system has progressed a lot since my father's time, and I am sure there would now be provisions in place to continue his education, but at that time the long-term effect of him missing school left him being treated as mentally disabled as well as physically disabled. This would be traumatic enough for any child, but also during this period his father was killed and his mother was confined to an institution, unable to continue functioning due to the grief of losing her husband.

After many years in a wheelchair then calipers, against the odds my father finally managed to walk, despite being told by doctors this would never happen. This to me implies the first signs of a growth mindset.

Fortunately, my grandfather's sister, Aunty Annie, a spinster with a wonderful heart, took my father in and he finally started to have a semblance of a normal life. He got a job in the shipyards and also bluffed the papers so he could do his national service.

The Glasgow shipyards in the 1960s had a strong union presence. While the unions did a great job to protect the workers, they were also a breeding ground for a fixed mindset of how things should or should not be done.

It was a decision my father made with a fixed mindset that proved to be one of the biggest regrets of his life. Despite his early educational setbacks, he was a quick learner with a smart mind and had become an accomplished draftsman. Because of his skills and ability to teach he was offered a job as a lecturer at Clydebank College. This could have given my family an opportunity to move from our council high-rise flat to a 'bought house' as they call it where I'm from. But whether it was 'Imposter Syndrome' (see page 131) or a fixed mindset holding him back, possibly a combination of both, he didn't think he could do it which led to him turning the job down.

Fast forward to 1990. My father was 55 years old and 'times were a-changing', computers were all the rage, and the shipbuilding industry was slowing down with lots of manufacturing moving overseas. Jobs were decreasing and skill sets were changing. With the introduction of 'AutoCAD', a new era was born. The older men who could only draw on boards were being replaced with the new kids on the block who were a whiz on AutoCAD. My dad was left with a choice: he could either keep his fixed mindset, moan and complain that it wasn't fair and that he was too old to learn new skills, or he could revisit the growth mindset from his youth and go to night school and learn new skills which would secure his employment for years to come. Yep, you've guessed it, at age 55 a mature student was born. It was exhausting for him, as his health had never fully recovered from his youth and arthritis had well and truly set in, but he persevered and achieved his Higher National Diploma.

By learning from his previous mistake of turning down the lecturer role, he decided he could do anything he wanted and moved into the contractor world, which not only paid better but meant that with his draft board and AutoCAD combination ability he became one of the most sought-after draftsmen in Scotland and the North of England. His effort and attitude to learning ensured he maximised the rest of his working life.

Many lesser men did not take the opportunity to retrain and never regained employment, blaming employers and the environment for not being able to return to work.

So is mindset nature or nurture? I don't feel educated enough on the subject to give you a definitive answer, but as with most subjects, I have an opinion. I think it is a combination of both, and as we see from my dad's example it can fluctuate.

For me it's all about growth, so where does my mindset come from? My parents ALWAYS rewarded me for effort, an example being my 'O level' (similar to GCSE) results. Being a second sibling to my academic sister, Norma, my parents hoped I would follow in her footsteps. However, being an undiagnosed dyslexic put paid to that.

When it came to the results day, the only positive result on the certificate was a C for arithmetic. Was I berated for poor results? Far from it, and my house was full of cards and flowers from well-wishers congratulating me on my efforts. How did they know? Because my parents had total belief that I did my best, and despite the overall result were proud enough of me to tell friends, family and neighbours.

My parents quickly understood that academia was not my 'thing' but always supported me to persevere until I found the thing that made my heart sing. I think they were shocked when I left home at 20 to travel the world on my own, but they never once held me back from carving out my own destiny. As a parent now myself I can see how worried they must have been, but they never shared their fears with me.

I finally found it was sales and entrepreneurism that made my heart sing. Both are full of ups and downs, and it is easy for a fixed mindset to try to creep in, especially on the dark days when things don't go your way, so you need to have a growth mindset to succeed.

So, what are my top tips for a positive mindset?

1. Surround yourself with the right people

Since they passed away, I sadly no longer have my parents to support me, but I have a core group of business friends who are always on hand to listen and keep me focused on the positive. Be around people who genuinely get a buzz from your success, not people who feel threatened by it. Who supports *you*?

2. We are not all great at everything, we all make mistakes

I love mistakes, and I am frequently heard saying, "Yeah, that's another chapter for my book". The key is to learn from mistakes. The definition of insanity is making the same mistake over and over and expecting different results, to quote Albert Einstein. So write a list of your mistakes and some action points on what you can do not to repeat them.

3. Challenge yourself

I used to use the fact I am dyslexic as an excuse to say that writing was not for me. I now regularly write a blog and, as you know, I have even written a book. Thankfully, people feel inspired by what I have to say. What have you always wanted to do, but feel you can't? Maybe it is just a mindset issue that is holding you back from reaching your dreams.

4. Know your why

Having your own business can be one of the most rewarding and frustrating things in the world. Over the years it has frequently crossed my mind to jack it in and get a 'proper' job. Dig deep, persevere and reflect on the reason you set up the business in the first place. For me, I know small businesses need me to teach them to sell, it is my purpose and torch in the dark moments. What is your purpose?

5. Keep learning new things

Thanks to Carol Dweck's research I have gained more knowledge on a new subject which I can now share with my audience. When was the last time you expanded your knowledge?

Whether you agree with me that mindset is nature, nurture or both, I think it's something that is essential if you are to be successful. You have to have that ability to pick out the positives from the negatives, it's what spurs you on in moments of darkness. Anyone who has started a business can tell you that it is no mean feat, but if you stick with it, it's worth every minute of heartbreak you'll experience on the way. You have the potential to be one of the STARS, and all you need is to adopt a growth mindset. Easier said than done, I know. But don't give up, trust me, it's worth it in the end.

The Difference Between Sales and Marketing

One of my biggest frustrations in life is that very few people know the difference between sales and marketing. I will ask someone about their sales strategy and more often than not they will start telling me about their marketing plan. Although sales and marketing are linked there is a difference and I think it's important you know this.

As I have mentioned, golf once played a big part of my life. Here's a little golf analogy I like to use to explain the difference between the two. Marketing put the tee in the ground and the ball on the tee. Salespeople then hit the ball up the fairway, put it on the green and putt it in the hole. At this point a marketer usually says, "No, that's not right, marketing put the tee in the ground and the ball on the tee, we knock it up the fairway and put it right up to the pin, then you sales guys come along, tap it in and take all the glory."

Whichever way you choose to look at it, one couldn't happen without the other. Typically, anything related to promotion is considered a marketing activity, for example, adverts, social media posts and email campaigns. Something like networking is a bit trickier to classify. I believe it to be a sales activity as you go with the intention of selling yourself and building relationships, however, others will argue that it's a marketing activity because it's a form of promotion. I like to think that anything which involves human-to-human interaction is sales. After all, this is usually when the sales process begins (you'll learn more about this later).

As if it wasn't confusing enough, the rise of the internet has made it even more difficult to explain. I see it like this: anything that is sold online, for example when you buy something from Amazon, is a hole-in-one for marketing. No human interaction has been made, therefore marketing takes the win.

As there is no clearcut line between sales and marketing, my advice to you is decide for yourself which activities fall under which category, otherwise it'll get messy.

An Overview of The Four Key Pillars of Sales

I have broken down the art of selling into four pillars. This gives us a chance to look at each of the different aspects in a little more detail and discuss some of the scenarios which may result at the different stages.

I have talked about how I created the methodology around the STARS, but what does it look like to you?

I have called this 'The Four Key Pillars of Sales'. Why four pillars? Having a pillar in each corner spreads the load and builds a strong foundation from which to grow.

Pillar 1: Behaviours

Ultimately people buy people. Have you ever wondered why you cannot stand some people, yet you can make an instant connection with others? Like finds like. It is easy to sell to the people like you, but what about those that aren't? The trick is to identify your customer's behaviour and adapt to build a strong relationship.

Pillar 2: Process

Sales IS a process. There is a businessman you may have heard of… James Dyson. For those who don't know, he makes vacuum cleaners. They go through a manufacturing process, but occasionally some will fail quality control. This is like sales – you will never sell to everyone, but if you follow the process you will sell to a lot more.

Pillar 3: Strategy

I challenge business owners to explain their sales strategy and most of the time they tell me their marketing strategy or business plan. So why not a sales strategy? How are you supposed to know where you're going if you don't know what you are trying to achieve? Without a strategy, you will be in the dark and struggle to move in the right direction.

Pillar 4: Confidence

People tell me, 'I can't sell' or 'I don't like selling', and if I had a pound for every time someone said this, I would have retired to my villa in the South of France by now. The truth is they don't know how to sell and therefore lack confidence. If you aren't confident when you're selling, your customers won't be confident when buying. When you understand the behaviours, know the process and have a strategy, confidence comes naturally.

PILLAR ONE

UNDERSTANDING CUSTOMER BEHAVIOURS

In sales there are two things you need to know, your behaviour and that of your customers. Once you understand your own behaviour, it becomes easy to adapt and build relationships with those who are not like you. As I said, like finds like, it is easy to sell to people who are like you. But it's those who go the extra mile to learn how to be a chameleon who reap the rewards.

Have you ever met someone you didn't like? Yes. Me too. It's a simple fact that we don't get on with everyone, and this is because we have different views of the world. I am not a psychologist, therefore I use the DISC model created by William Moulton Marston and the psychology from Carl Jung's studies to explain how we have different behaviours which impact the way we interpret and react to situations. There are lots of behaviour models and tools out there, but the reason I use this one is because it's simple and easy to follow.

The image below shows there are four behaviours: red, yellow, green and blue. We are of course a mix of all the colours, not just one. After all, if we were all the same the world would be dull.

There are tools which can help determine your behaviours. (For instance, I am an Ensize practitioner and therefore use Ensize when working with my clients.)

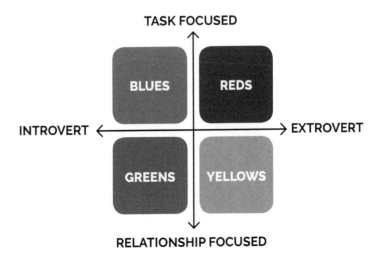

Let's start by looking at the different behaviour types. To help you understand I'm going to take you back to school for a moment. I'm going to give you a 30-minute English test, but don't worry, it's hypothetical.

Imagine yourself in a room full of 30 pupils under test conditions, and this will help you grasp the idea of the different behaviour types.

Task-focused Extroverts

First up, we have the task-focused extroverts, or as we like to call them… the Reds!

Now imagine you're doing an English test at school, someone who is red will have their hand up within 20 minutes, saying 'Miss Miss, I've finished already, what's taking everyone so long?' At this point a Red is thinking 'check me out', and will be using their hands to do the loser sign to all of their classmates. Does this remind you of anyone?

Reds are great at getting the task done fast, but they lack concentration to ensure it is done properly. That same Red that finished the test early will get the paper back on results day and say, 'Oh, I didn't realise there was another side to that paper'. They are more concerned with finishing the task and looking good than with the actual result.

Relationship-focused Extroverts

Next, we have the relationship-focused extroverts, also known as… the Yellows!

Let's go back to the classroom, where the Yellows are easily distracted and find it difficult to stay on task. 10 minutes into the test, they will be chatting and giggling at the back of the classroom, more concerned with the party they have been invited to at the weekend than the test, saying 'Oops, sorry Miss, I was talking to Denise about who's going to the party and what I'm going to wear!'

Yellows love attention and can often be perceived as being loud and disruptive. Their excitable nature along with a short attention span means they move at a very fast pace, they usually take the conversation off topic and they speak at a million miles an hour.

Relationship-focused Introverts

Now, we have the relationship-focused introverts, more commonly known as… the Greens!

Greens are the quiet ones, they often lack confidence to speak up, and when they do their tone will be low and whispery, their words will be slow and hesitant. Although they are introverts, they are also relationship focused, and, taking you back to the classroom again, this means the Greens will be more concerned about their friend Deborah with a headache. In this situation, a Green is likely to put their hand up and say, 'Excuse me Miss, I know we have a test but my friend Deborah has a headache and I think I should take her to the nurse'. A Green will then take the friend to the nurse without the class even noticing they've gone.

We all need friends like this, ones that care and put others first. However, Greens aren't perfect and they can test your patience, as they are known to be very indecisive.

Task-focused Introverts

Finally, we have the task-focused introverts, and we call these… the Blues!

Attention to detail is key for Blues, and they strive for perfection in everything they do. In our classroom scenario, the Blues will be the ones that go through the test over and over again, utilising every minute of their time. They will make sure every 'i' is dotted and every 't' is crossed.

The Blues are similar to the Greens, shy away from attention and would much prefer to sit on their own in a corner working away than interact with the rest of the class.

It's Not Rocket Science

Now I have given you a brief introduction to the behaviours as defined by DISC profiling, I am going to delve deeper, showing you how you can implement this in your business to build stronger relationships and increase sales.

Before we get into the nitty-gritty it is important to remember that we are a mix of all the colours, but we all have one or two that are more dominant than the others. If you hadn't already worked it out, I'm a Yellow/Red or an Orange as I like to call it. Hence why I adore being The Entrepreneur's Godmother and absolutely love sales!

Knowing the four behaviour types helps us to understand how we are all different and respond to situations differently, even if we're from the same family. Haven't you ever wondered how you can be the polar opposite of your brother or sister? Every behaviour has its good and bad days, it's like Yin and Yang; our good qualities can also manifest themselves as traits that aren't so attractive. Understanding behaviours will help you adapt to those who aren't like you, enabling you to sell more.

The Reds

Reds are the leaders of the pack and will often strive for management roles. They are the task-focused extroverts, and this makes them quick decision makers and problem solvers, as they often act fast and think later. They want to get the job done and they are competitive so will seek out challenges and compete with their peers to prove they are the best at what they do.

Reds want results. They don't necessarily care what the result is but they want it fast and they want it now. A keyword to listen out for when identifying a Red is 'when' – they will ask questions such as:

- When can I have it?

- When will I see a return?

- When do you want to meet?

They are very time sensitive and scared of failure, therefore will take the initiative to complete the task. Although they dislike it, when they do fail they learn their lesson, and it makes them more determined to get it right next time.

As a natural leader, a Red finds it easy to delegate, although this can often come across as being demanding and controlling. They also find it difficult to listen to the views and opinions of others. Do you have that friend that asks for your advice, then completely ignores you and does their own thing? Yes, that friend is a Red!

We nickname the Reds the 'ticking time bombs'. They can be perceived as very aggressive and you never know when they are going to blow.

Alex Ferguson, the ex-Manchester United football team manager, is a good example of someone with Red characteristics. He led his team to win hundreds of matches, including thirteen premier league titles, five FA Cups and two UEFA Champion League titles, yet many will also remember him as the guy who allegedly threw a football boot at David Beckham's head.

When interacting with Reds there are two things you need to be aware of: there is a thin line between assertive and aggressive, and a thin line between confident and cocky, and the Reds don't often know where those lines are.

Selling to Reds

You know what to look for and how to spot them, but how do you adapt and sell to them. For those of you that are Green, selling to a Red will be your biggest challenge. We know that Reds are task focused and want results, and this can be good from the salesperson's perspective as they will give you a quick answer. They won't leave you to chase them for months but will tell you upfront 'yes' or 'no'. Their fast decision-making skill is a bonus when selling to them, but it also means you have to be quick. They don't want to know the ins and outs of everything, they need to know what it is, when they can have it and when they will reap the rewards. This is why the Greens may struggle. Remember, Reds are impatient and if you drag things out they will lose interest.

They can be confrontational and like to take control, but as the person selling to them, YOU need to be in control. This means you need to walk in and confidently pitch to them, keeping it short and sharp. You need to lead the dance and control the conversation by asking the right questions. Don't wait for them to ask you, ask them "When would you like it by?" This will sway a Red as they will see you are serious about delivering to their time schedule and demands.

A top tip for selling to a Red is NEVER ask to 'meet for coffee'. So many people ask me this and, as a Red, I can tell you it drives me up the wall. To me my time is precious, as it is to most Reds, so if you want to sell them something or collaborate tell them in an email or over the phone. Reds always want to know the purpose of the meeting, and if they think it has no value they will just palm you off. That's why as the seller you have to take the lead.

One of my friends, Jane, runs her own PR company and as a favour I introduced her to a client, Mike, who wanted help. Mike is a full blown Red and Jane is a Green, and during their original meeting Mike came up with lots of ideas of what he wanted to achieve. Jane in response said, 'That would be really nice, but I don't know if that's very realistic.' In Jane's eyes she was managing expectations, but in Mike's eyes Jane was being negative. When it came to writing a proposal, Mike wanted it the next day. Jane couldn't understand the urgency and it took her a week to get the proposal to (by this point a very impatient) Mike. After some negotiating, contracts were signed and they were in business. Mike expected weekly progress updates from Jane, but this was something she struggled to provide. She found it difficult to deliver to Mike's schedule and understand his viewpoint. In the end, she lost the contract and they both lost out because neither could adapt.

The Yellows

As relationship-focused extroverts, Yellows are great team builders and motivators, and they enjoy working with lots of people and communicating. You will always meet a Yellow at a networking event. Their energy is infectious and they can often make you feel very good about yourself, but be careful as they will have a bigger impact on you than you will on them. They lack concentration and find it really hard to stay on topic, and they are so busy flitting from one person to the next, there is a good chance they will forget all about you. We often compare Yellows to Dory, the fish from *Finding Nemo*, as they are easily distracted. Because of this, they find it difficult to see a task through to the end, and I call them half-a-job Harry.

Yellows love people and love attention, therefore they are always concerned with 'who' – they will ask:

- Who do you know?

- Who is that?

- Who's going with you?

They are very well connected because they are constantly asking for introductions and networking. If you want to get your name out there, befriend a Yellow, they will quite literally shout about you from the rooftops.

Often perceived as upbeat and energetic, Yellows can often come across as careless and self-centred, as they are more interested in who just walked in than what you've been trying to talk to them about for the last 15 minutes. We compare Yellows to a roller-coaster: when they are up they are all the way up, and when they are down they hit rock bottom, but they bounce back quickly.

A brilliant example of a Yellow is Taylor Swift. She's probably not the person you immediately think of but you only have to take a look at her social media presence to see it. She's known for two things: one, being one of the world's biggest pop singers, and two, her squad. For those of you who don't know about Taylor's squad, it's what she calls her group of friends, and unlike a regular person, her squad includes some of the world's most talented and wealthy young women. Every young star on the rise wants to be associated with Swifty, and if that doesn't scream Yellow, I don't know what does.

Selling to Yellows

The biggest challenge when selling to a Yellow is getting them to stand still long enough for you to tell them about your business. The key to selling to a Yellow is to keep it simple: if you overload them with information they will get bored and stop listening. For those of you who are Blue, you will find it hard to build a relationship with a Yellow. Yellows often view Blues as boring. So, keep the detail to a minimum and you'll stand a better chance of converting the sale.

Another thing to be wary of when trying to sell to a Yellow is their ability to keep you dangling on a thread. A lot of the time they will forget about you and palm you off saying, 'Yes, it is on my list of things to do'. You need to keep their head in the game. Don't be afraid to follow-up with an email reiterating the points of your initial discussion. And don't be offended if you have to re-introduce yourself next time you meet them.

Yellows make you feel good, so it is easy to get caught up in their crazy whirlwind. As a result, you will find you keep chasing them for the sale even when you know they are not a good fit for your product or service. Don't get caught up. They are great to be associated with but do not let them waste your time.

Status is important to Yellows – they love things that draw attention to themselves. The Yellows are the kind of people who buy a pair of shoes because they saw Kim Kardashian wearing similar ones in *Cosmo*. Yellows are easily impressed – if you have a large or well-known client, tell a Yellow and they are much more likely to buy into your product or service, just so they can tell their friends.

A great example of this is when one of my double-glazing clients tried selling to a Yellow. I was working with the sales executive to go through all the sales they had lost over a certain time period and decided to call the potential customers to see why they had not purchased. I phoned one lady, and when asked why she didn't buy she said, 'The man was boring, telling me about thermal values and measurements. I only wanted new windows because Doreen at number 4 had hers done'. My client is Blue and his customer was Yellow, and this is a perfect example of how overloading a Yellow with information can lose you a sale. It also demonstrates just how much Yellows are willing to buy something because someone else has bought it!

The Greens

Reliable and caring, you will often find Greens in people-orientated roles, such as HR, counsellors and GPs. They are very harmonious and can have a calming effect on people. They are great listeners, taking on board everyone's views and opinions, making them nice to have in an office environment. Greens are patient and appreciate that a good job takes time, and although they are relationship-focused they have the ability to stay focused and complete a task to the best of their ability. This has earned them the nickname 'the patient one'.

Greens seek security and safety in all aspects of their lives, hence why they fear change. It can take a Green a long time to adjust to something new, no matter how minor the change. Change can often make them feel threatened and insecure, and as a result they will avoid it at all costs.

Something key to listen out for when identifying a Green is the word 'why', and their caring nature means they often ask questions such as:

- Why do you feel like that?

- Why did you decide to do that?

- Why do think this is?

They want to know the story behind someone. They don't just want to know about you and your business; they want to build a genuine relationship and get to know you.

As you can probably guess, a Green will try to avoid conflict. However, on the rare occasion they do become involved, they find it very hard to control their emotions, they get nervous, and they can come across as an aggressive Red. Greens can find it hard to convey their feelings at the best of times, which means their words often come across as slow and unclear, making conflict extremely difficult for them.

You will struggle to find a Green in the spotlight because they dislike the attention.

Selling to Greens

Greens can be very indecisive and hesitant, making them difficult to sell to. For someone like a Red or Yellow, they may find selling to a Green quite a challenge. To adapt to a Green, you need to slow down the pace, slow your talking and slow the sales process. They do not like to be rushed or feel like they are being forced to purchase something. Be careful not to intimidate them, try to use a soft gentle tone when speaking, and give them time to think when you ask questions.

In case you haven't figured it out by now, sales is all about building relationships and establishing trust with your customers. This is even more so the case when selling to a Green. You really have to take an interest in them, get to know them; it is important for a Green to build genuine relationships. If you want them to buy, you need to take time to learn what they like, dislike, need and want. The sales process with a Green can be slow, but like a Yellow, they will recommend you to all their friends if they like you.

Greens are slow decision-makers; this may drive you a bit mad if you're trying to sell to them. You will have to walk them through every step of the process, which can be very time-consuming. But the most irritating thing is their inability to say 'no'. A Green doesn't want to hurt your feelings so will struggle to turn your offer down, and instead they will let you chase them for months. Be careful, as you could be wasting your time. A good way to overcome this is to test their commitment to the purchase (I will tell you more about this in pillar 2).

Another thing to be wary of when selling to Greens is their need for support when making decisions. Very rarely will a Green buy something there and then, but will want to take time to think about it and consult a trusted party. I always hear Green customers say, 'I really like it, and I will talk to my partner and come back to you'. They find it difficult to make the decision on their own. They need someone to back them up. A good way to overcome this is to find out whose opinion they value and try to include them from the start. Other than that all you can do is be patient and give them time; if you rush them they will feel threatened and you will lose the sale.

As a sales trainer and networking queen, I come across Greens all the time. I met one lady at a networking event who was interested in attending one of my workshops. But she was a Green, so instead of booking there and then, she said, 'I will go and speak to my husband and see what he thinks'. My team followed up and again she said the same. After a couple of months my team and I got a bit fed up, so we phoned her again to book her on a course and she said, 'I really want to come, I just need to check I can make that date'. Ok, well, fair enough we thought. To cut a long story short, it was nearly two years before she finally booked and came to the workshop. When adapting to a Green, perseverance and patience is key. She really was interested in attending but she just needed to do things at her own pace.

It's not that Greens don't want things as badly as Reds or Yellows, it's just their thoughtfulness and pace hold them back. For example, if they found themselves in a room with Tom Cruise, deep down if they were a fan they would really want a selfie. But by the time they pluck up the courage to ask, the Red would have already taken one and the Yellow would have wangled an invite to his L.A. home.

The Blues

A stickler for the rules, Blues are the types of people to actually read the terms and conditions. They crave detail and want to know every aspect of something, not only that but they want proof. You can't just tell a Blue that something is great, they need the facts, figures and evidence to back it up. Blues are very logical, and this is what makes them so task-focused. They like to prioritise and ensure everything is done in the correct order. A Blue is not the type of person to order something from IKEA and throw away the assembly instructions, they will read them from cover to cover before they even begin to think about assembling. The positive of this is that they get the job done right first time.

Blues are the perfectionists, always looking for mistakes and holes. A keyword to listen out for when trying to identify a Blue is 'how'. They will ask:

- How do you know that is true?

- How do you know it works?

- How do you plan on achieving that?

And trust me, they will want a heavily detailed answer, as there's no fast-tracking when it comes to a Blue.

Being task-focused means they can be great to have on a project as they keep everyone performing on time to the highest of quality. However, they are introverts and often struggle with emotional and irrational behaviour. When talking to a Blue, unless it is something they are really interested in, you can expect minimal conversation and yes/no answers. You really need to find common ground if you want to get them talking, but be careful, once they start it can be hard to get them to stop.

Due to their inability to break the rules, the Blues are often called 'the red-tapist'. You will often find them in data handling and information processing roles in the accounting, IT and law sectors.

Selling to Blues

Let me be upfront with you. As a typical Yellow, I get bored easily and find it really hard to communicate with high-detail Blues. So, for all you Yellow readers out there, this will be your biggest challenge. My top tip is to be prepared. If you know you are going to be selling to a Blue do your preparation. Put your pitch together and have the facts and figures to back everything up, and if you are going to make a statement about how your product or service can change their life, prove it. A good way to do this is by sharing detailed client case studies. Facts and statistics are key, as Blues really like numbers. When you are telling them about the ROI they could get from investing in you, use percentages, graphs and tables.

Give them something to take away, Blues aren't the types to rush in without weighing up the pros and cons and doing research. Have a proposal of some kind that they can take away and refer back to when making a decision. But be accurate; if you get things wrong or don't know your numbers a Blue will pull you up on it. Always take notes when speaking to them, as they will remember what they told you two months ago and will expect you to remember too. When you give them something like a proposal, make sure you have included everything you discussed. If you have missed something they will only come back and ask you to include it.

Blues can be very pedantic about things. When I launched The Entrepreneur's Godmother brand at one of the UK's largest sales exhibitions, I was invited to give a presentation. This was nothing new for me as I often public speak in front of a large audience. At the end, there was a queue of people waiting to ask me questions, and I eventually got to this one man who had been waiting for around 20 minutes to speak to me. He was clearly a Blue and the only reason he wanted to talk to me was to tell me there was a spelling mistake in my presentation. I was surprised that someone was so bothered about a misspelt word that they would wait in a queue for 20 minutes to tell me. To this day I remember the misspelt word – I had written 'loose' instead of 'lose'. If a Blue sees a mistake they will tell you.

Body Language – Uncovering the Clues

You don't necessarily need to speak to someone to work out their behaviour. We give a lot away by our actions, and I can tell by someone's body language what colour they are. When I delivered training in Kuwait, some of the women had their faces covered, but even when I could only see their eyes, I knew their behaviour colour.

It is always good to know what you're walking into. If you are at an event and you are looking around the room for someone to speak to, instead of going in all guns blazing, take a step back and try and analyse their behaviour from their actions. That way you will already have the upper hand, you will know what colour to adapt to and how to approach them.

According to science, up to 93% of our communication is non-verbal with only 7% being verbal (Morgan, 2015). The majority of body language is unconscious and, as humans, we are not even aware of the non-verbal clues we give out. How crazy is that? This just shows how much you can learn from someone's body language if you really take the time to stop and observe.

So, what are the key giveaways for identifying someone through their body language? Let me tell you.

Interpreting Red Body Language

Someone with Red behaviour will often have their arms crossed, with straight posture, almost making them look bigger. This is to display their authority. Their task-focused nature means they are always keeping an eye on the time, so if you see someone keep checking their watch, it is probably because they are Red and thinking about all the other things they should be doing.

Other signs might be leaning in; this can often make people feel a little inferior, but take it as a buying sign. On the other hand, if a Red has become disengaged, they will probably start looking at their phone, checking their emails and getting on with what they deem to be more important. Remember Reds like attention, they are the type in the gym to huff and puff really loudly so that everyone can hear them and see how great they are, or huff and puff in the office so that everyone knows they are having a bad day.

Interpreting Yellow Body Language

Yellows are all smiles, and jazz hands. These guys are tactile and will often hug you or give you air kisses (yes, I plead guilty to all of these!). In a room of people, Yellows like to be front and centre. If they aren't getting any immediate attention they might be looking out the window and round the room. They can also be a bit absent-minded and forget to switch their text notifications off. And, talking of phones, they can usually be found taking selfies. They like to be surrounded by people and may get bored being stuck with their own company for too long.

Interpreting Green Body Language

This can be a little trickier, purely because Greens aren't always easy to spot. They are usually hiding amongst the crowd or tucked away in a corner. A perfect example of a Green at an event would be someone standing at the edge of the room, arms crossed and looking anywhere but at you. They may even pretend to be busy faffing with something to try and avoid talking to you. Greens crossing their arms is an example of closed body language. This signals to someone that they feel a little bit threatened by the situation and crossing their arms acts as a barrier. Greens can also look as though they are shrinking into themselves, making themselves look as small as possible.

Interpreting Blue Body Language

Another group that avoids eye contact are the Blues. They have a logical approach and desire for facts. They can be perceived as being aloof and standoffish and are considered to be poker-faced. But don't be fooled, the grey matter will be whirring away.

Next time you attend an event, I challenge you to take a couple of minutes to stand and observe those around you and see if you can identify their behaviour. You will be surprised at how much you can interpret about someone just from their body language.

Understanding Behaviours Online

When I started out in sales there was no such thing as the internet. Wow, now I do sound old. In today's world the internet is prevalent in everything we do, especially social media. There are over 3.5 billion internet users across the world (Statista, 2017a), of which 2.46 billion are on social media (Statista, 2017b). If you are starting a business or already have a business and aren't on social media, why not? My advice to you is get online and start connecting.

Since day one, I have always used social media to grow and connect with my audience. Facebook, LinkedIn, Twitter and Instagram are amazing platforms for growing brand awareness. The majority of us use social media every day to talk to people and use it to build customer relationships, but how can we build strong effective relationships with people we may never meet? Simple, use the behaviours. By now you should know enough about the colours to have a basic understanding of each behaviour. So how does that translate when it is online?

Like body language, someone's social media profile gives away a lot about them. I'll use LinkedIn as an example as I think this is the easiest platform to use when trying to identify someone's colour.

Identifying Reds Online

In their profile photos men will often be wearing open-collared shirts, and women will be professionally dressed and usually have formal make-up. A Red will be looking directly into the camera, and usually have quite a stern authoritative look on their face. They will want to dominate the photo, making themselves the object of focus. As a result there will be little background to distract your attention, and if there is a background it will usually be plain.

Now you know how to spot them, here is the best way to get a Red engaged in conversation.

A message should:

- be specific and to the point

- be short and snappy

- avoid too much detail

- avoid small talk

- not use emojis

Remember what I said earlier about asking Reds to meet for coffee, and keep that in mind when starting a conversation online. They would much prefer that you be upfront with them and tell them what you really want. For example, if you were connecting with me (a typical Red) on LinkedIn you could say this:

> *Hi Alison, I really liked your profile and see that you won at the GB Entrepreneur of the Year Awards. I think there's something we could work on together as I have connections who could benefit from your services. When are you available for a 15-minute chat?*

Try and big them up but get to the point fast. If you waffle they will lose interest. Also, try and advance the communication offline and get talking over the phone, as they will get fed up messaging back and forth. Be time specific because they are task-focused.

Identifying Yellows Online

A typical Yellow's profile photo will be a selfie of them on holiday with a glass of wine or cocktail in hand. The photo tends to be quite close-up and they will usually be pouting or posing. Yellows tend to look less professional in their photos. It's usually a photo of them having fun on holiday.

When sending a message to a Yellow:

- keep it short because as we know they lose concentration

- use friendly language

- show that you're enthusiastic and eager – they don't like boring people

- avoid formalities

Here's an example of what you could say when messaging a yellow:

> *Hi Charlie, your profile looks brilliant, well done with all the great work you're doing. I see that you know Hannah. I met her last month at an event, she's hilarious. There's so much stuff we could do together, it would be great fun. When are you free to meet up for a drink and have a chat?*

A top tip, remember that Yellows are all about 'who', so if you have a mutual contact or can namedrop, do it. They are always looking to have a good time, so try to keep it relatively light and upbeat.

Identifying Greens Online

As we know Greens try and hide, so that's why they will usually use a photo of themselves with friends and family, so they are not the main focus. Sometimes they will even use photos of themselves with their pets. They may even have the dreaded grey egg, which is the basic default profile photo on social media. The Greens will have lots of background in their picture for example, it will usually be a long/wide shot of them, and could even be a group photo with other people in it. Again, this is an attempt to take the focus off them. Being naturally caring, they tend to have smiley and friendly expressions on their face.

Although Greens are the quiet, shy types, they are relationship-focused and love meeting new people, so just remember when sending a message to:

- avoid being over-enthusiastic as they are easily intimidated

- use friendly language

- take interest in them

- avoid being pushy

- give them time to reply, don't make them feel rushed

Unlike Reds, the Greens love meeting people for coffee, so when you message you could say this:

> *Hi Nicola, I really like your profile, I would love to know more about you and your business. It would be great to get to know you better and see if there is anything we can do together. Would you like to meet for a coffee?*

Remember, Greens want to build genuine relationships because they really care about people, so it's okay to say, "How are you?" and ask more questions outside of business. If they have kids they will definitely want to talk about them. Just one thing to be wary of is that a Green may not want to meet after one message, so maybe ask to meet after you've messaged back and forth a bit.

Identifying Blues Online

If you hadn't already guessed it, a photo of a Blue is very formal, men will be wearing a shirt buttoned up to the top and a tie that's neat and tight. Women will be in formal wear but it will be plain, for example, a basic white blouse and tailored black jacket. Blues tend to avoid eye contact with the camera. They will either have a portrait photo of them looking away or a photo of them at their desk working. Again, like the Greens they won't want to be the focus so will hide where they can.

Now, we know Blues have an eye for detail and like lots of information, so when sending them a message through social media, remember to:

- clearly state the purpose

- provide them with some background (perhaps of who you are)

- use formal language

- avoid using emojis and slang terms

- try and use facts

A message to a Blue is likely to be longer than a message you would send to any other colour; for example, if I was sending a message to a Blue, I would say:

> *Dear Sue, I'm Alison, The Entrepreneur's Godmother and I provide sales training and coaching to startups, micros and owner-managed businesses. Studies published in Entrepreneur magazine show staff training can increase productivity by 30%. After reading your profile I see you have previously engaged with training providers. I think there is potential for us to collaborate. When are you free to discuss this further?*

Notice how the message is very formal and I have given more background on myself than I did when messaging other colours. Also note the use of the language and how I have referred back to their profile, which shows them that I read it and haven't just randomly messaged them.

Adapting is Not Acting

At one of the first ever workshops I delivered a man came up to me at the end, and I could already tell he was quite Green. He explained how he was really nervous about attending the workshop and had to stop several times on the way because he felt ill as he was overcome with nerves. He said to me, "Wow, I always thought that pretending to be something I'm not was fake and phoney, but by understanding the behaviours I can see how adapting to others is essential for my business." Some people may say that you're being fake but actually you're treating someone in the way they want to be treated. We have been brought up to think we should "treat others how we would like to be treated" but I flip that on its head and say, treat others how they want to be treated, it's just good customer service. Also, that nervous guy is now a regular networker and his business has turned around.

Not an Exact Science

I am a strong believer in the colours and use them in every aspect of my life. However, it is not an exact science. I recently met a smiley, enthusiastic man at an event, and I could already tell he was a Yellow as he was telling me about his latest hobby, salsa dancing with his wife. You could have knocked me over with a feather when he said he was an accountant. Typically, we would consider accountants to be Blues, but not in this case. There are some people who don't fit in with the colours and some that are a mix of them all, and these are the ones that are really hard to figure out. Just remember, although the colours are usually pretty spot on, there are always those that don't fit the mould.

PILLAR TWO

THE SALES PROCESS

Before we get into the detail of the sales process, there are a couple of things I want to go over with you.

The first thing is the difference between business-to-business, also known as B2B, and business-to-consumer, often referred to as B2C. This is something I will talk more and more about as we go on, so it's important you know the difference between the two. B2B is when one business sells to another, for example, I am a business owner and I provide a service to other businesses, therefore I am B2B. The other side is B2C, and an example of this is all of your high street shops where you are a consumer and they sell a product or service to you. These days a lot of B2C selling is done online, and going back to what I said about the difference between marketing and sales, this is a hole-in-one for marketing.

Buying Motives

The second thing I would like to go over with you is why people buy. The behaviours helped us understand who our customers are, but why do they buy a particular product or service? We call these the buying motives, and there are five key motives, one of which is behind every sale:

1. Prestige

2. Price

3. Offers

4. Continuity

5. Competition

Prestige

This is when someone buys something because of the perception that comes with it, for example, when one of your friends buys a BMW because they think it gives people the illusion they are successful and well-off. The purpose of a car is to get us from A to B, it's not necessary to have a BMW or Jaguar. It's the same with clothes – we all need clothes but we don't all need Armani or Gucci. Going back to the behaviours, this is a typical Yellow or Red move.

Price

When it comes to sales, price is the most common objection. Everyone says they buy on price, meaning they buy the cheapest products. However, this isn't strictly true. If it was, you would see tons of people walking round the supermarket with trolleys full of white labelled products. Let's be honest, this doesn't happen very often because the majority of us would rather spend a little bit more on something that tastes nice rather than something that tastes like a cardboard cake. There are people who have no choice but to buy on the price, for example, low income families will buy white label products to stretch their budget further.

Offers

Most people get this confused with price, but it's slightly different. When you buy something on special offer you usually buy a premium product that you wouldn't usually buy because it's 2 for 1 or half price. Take McVitie's Jaffa Cakes as an example. They are the premium orange flavoured cake in supermarkets and probably something that isn't on your weekly shopping list – instead you'll buy the supermarket brand of orange flavoured cake. But when the Jaffa cakes are on offer for £1 you'll buy them instead because in your head you're getting a bargain, even though your standard orange flavoured cakes are still only 90p.

Continuity

This is when someone continually buys the same brand, which can be down to brand loyalty but also habit. It's a bit like when someone only buys Heinz Ketchup because that's what their mum bought when they were wee and they wouldn't have their fish and chips any other way. Greens dislike change, therefore tend to be continuity buyers.

Competition

This is something that is more common in B2B businesses. This is when one company buys something because one of their competitors did. For example, when I launched my business I did it at one of the UK's biggest sales exhibitions, but the only reason I did this was because one of my competitors was exhibiting and I wanted to be seen on the same par. It's a little bit like how Instagram and Facebook integrated 'stories' because they saw it as a popular feature on Snapchat.

Hierarchy of Authority

Hopefully you're still with me, I know this is a lot to take in, but it's all really valuable if you want to be able to sell and have a successful business. The third thing we need to discuss is the hierarchy. Before you start selling to someone you need to make sure you're selling to the right person. More often than not, one of my team will attend a networking event and someone will try to get them to sign up for a paid membership, without even taking the time to ask if they have the authority to make that decision. If they did, they would realise they are wasting their time because they need to be speaking to me and not one of my team.

The triangle diagram below gives you an idea of how a business hierarchy works. I'm going to talk you through each level:

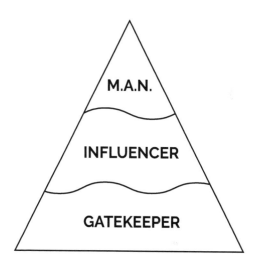

M.A.N.

Now don't panic ladies, I don't mean that a human of the male variety is always on top, for after all, we know that's not true. M.A.N. stands for Money, Authority, Needs, meaning this is the person who ultimately has the money to spend, the authority to make decisions and the need to be solved. This is the person who signs off on the sale, therefore the person you need to be negotiating with.

This is the part I see as one of the most common mistakes in B2B sales – not qualifying who's involved with the decision-making process. As part of the services I offer, I go on site with my clients to observe their sales skills. When I do this, I don't speak which is hard for me. I was on site with one client, Debra, who was doing a fantastic job following the process. But when she went to close, she realised the person she was meeting with was not the M.A.N. and did not have authority to buy. Had she known this in advance, she could have made sure the decision maker attended, or used the meeting to acquire information to set up another meeting with the M.A.N. It isn't always possible for the decision maker to be in the room, but you should always know who they are.

Influencers

Influencers don't necessarily have the power to make decisions but they do hold the power to sway the M.A.N.'s decision. It is likely that you will meet an influencer at an event. For example, when I send my team out, I send the influencers. They may have some power to persuade me into buying something, but don't waste your time giving influencers the full sales pitch because they don't actually have the authority to make the decision.

Gatekeepers

These guys are the protectors, guarding the M.A.N. at the top. Someone like a PA or Secretary can be considered a gatekeeper as they will only let you through when you can prove you have an appointment or that someone is expecting your call. Top tip, never lie to the gatekeeper, they will catch you out. One of my clients from a recruitment company once lied and said she wasn't from a recruitment company, but when she got through to the M.A.N. and revealed where she was calling from she had already lost the respect of the potential client.

If you are making a call and get stuck with the gatekeeper, how do you get past that person? Here are my Gold Dust Tips For Getting Past The Gatekeepers.

1. **Confidence**

   First and foremost, to get past the gatekeeper you need to have confidence. I've been a gatekeeper and now my team are my gatekeepers, and they can smell fear a mile away. If you stumble and say, "Ummm, can I speak to the person who deals with your... blah blah", they automatically know it's a sales call and will palm you off, saying, "Please can you send the information to info@..." If you're confident, the gatekeeper is more likely to have confidence in what you're saying and put you through to the M.A.N.

2. **Names**

Always use someone's name where you can. With LinkedIn and company websites it's easy to find out who heads up a department. You no longer have to say, "Can I speak to the person who deals with your so and so", you can say, "Hi, can you put me through to Jo Smith please". If you know the name of the person you want to speak to, it sounds like you have already established a relationship.

3. **Befriend the gatekeeper**

You want to build a good relationship with the gatekeeper. Going back to names, not only do you want the name of the M.A.N. but get the name of the gatekeeper. You can say, "Thank you and what was your name?", then say, "Oh thanks Jennifer, that's great." The next time you call them you can use their name and say, "Hi Jennifer, it's Alison again, can you put me through to Jo please?" This will help speed up the process next time.

If you still continue to struggle, gatekeepers usually work nine to five and take an hour's lunch break. Phoning outside of gatekeeper times means someone else will pick up the phone and it may be easier to get through.

4. **Name drop**

If you can't find the name of the M.A.N. but you know the name of someone else in the company, use it. You can say, "I usually deal with Sam in marketing but I don't think he's the right person to talk to." The gatekeeper will feel more comfortable letting you through as you already have a connection with the company.

5. Honesty is the best policy

Remember what I said about being honest, as it's really important. But there are situations where it can be hard to be honest, especially when the gatekeeper asks, "Is she expecting your call?" You don't want to lie if they aren't, but you can talk around it. If you've met them before you could say something along the lines of, "We met at a networking meeting last Friday and I was calling to follow-up on our discussion". Ideally you would have tried to contact the M.A.N. before calling – after all it's not 1984 and you don't need to cold call anymore. If you don't know the M.A.N. personally, you can send them a message on LinkedIn, then when you call and the gatekeeper starts asking questions, you can say, "I sent her a message on LinkedIn and I thought it would be easier to continue the discussion over the phone".

6. Leave a message

A question I often get asked is, should you leave a message with the gatekeeper or send an email to info@. My top tip is not to leave a message as it's very unlikely they will call you back, unless the message is compelling. An example of this was my conversation with a television production company. In the message, I mentioned a famous agent and TV channel which led them to call me back immediately. Remember this can't be a lie and it is an unusual occurrence to get a callback.

7. Fortune favours the brave

A lot of the time the gatekeeper will turn around and say, "She's not available at the moment as she's in a meeting". Now they could actually be in a meeting but there's a good chance they're not. Instead of giving the gatekeepers your details in the hope they phone you back, you can ask for the M.A.N.'s mobile number by saying, "That's fine, just give me her mobile number and I'll call her back later". Most people aren't confident enough to do this, but fortune favours the brave and sometimes it pays off.

Those are my Gold Dust Tips For Getting Past The Gatekeepers, so next time you're on the phone and get stuck with the secretary think of these seven tips. Sometimes the gatekeeper can be an inconvenience, but don't be too hard on them, they are only doing their job. Oh, remember, always makes notes of names and phone numbers so you have them for the future. And if the M.A.N. really is in a meeting, make sure you schedule a reminder to call back (we'll talk later about some great tools to help you keep on top of this).

The Sales Process

Now that we've gone over some of the basics, let's get down to business.

I can't imagine that when James Dyson invented his first vacuum cleaner he thought "I know, let's throw some stuff together and hope it works". To manufacture a product, you must have a foolproof process. You may have to tweak your ideas many times to achieve perfection, but it is by following a clear process that consistent results happen.

Sales, too, is a process, but many salespeople and business owners are not familiar with it. Excellent sales do not happen by accident, they come when you follow the process.

Lots of salespeople think they can close business deals with a big grin and a large address book. Without a full understanding of the sales process and customer journey, they have no idea what they can learn from and how to improve their skills. It's this lack of understanding which can cause erratic results. A salesperson won't sell to everyone, but by using the process they will certainly sell to more.

There are 10 steps to every sale, and these can be seen in the image below. Depending on what you're selling and who you're selling to there is no specified time for how long it should take to complete each step and make the sale. However, it goes without saying that the higher the value of the sale the longer the process. Going back to the colours, it may take you longer to sell something to a Green or Blue than it would to a Yellow or Red because the Greens and Blues take longer to make decisions.

It's imperative that you know the sales process. You don't have to necessarily use mine, but it works for me and it is a great starting point.

One thing that hasn't changed since time began is that people buy people. Remember how, in understanding behaviours, I spoke about getting on better with some people more than with others – maybe you don't like someone because they are always late or talk too much. Whatever it is, they do something that really annoys you.

This is because they haven't followed the process and taken the time to understand your behaviour. The reason we adapt and follow the process is to build relationships.

Even when someone does understand behaviours, there are things they may do that destroy the relationship, like forgetting someone's name or turning up unprepared. Knowing the process helps you to avoid these mistakes and build a strong bond with the customer.

Step 1: Be Prepared

The first step in the process is to be prepared. I know what you're thinking, 'That's easy, that's just common sense'. Well if that was true, why do so many people forget it? Sometimes it's easy to skip the simplest steps.

As the saying goes, "fail to prepare and prepare to fail". What do I mean by this? There are several small things that you can do before heading into a meeting or preparing for a call that will help make the process more seamless. Four questions I like to ask myself before any sales situation are: who? when? where? and what?

Who? If you're heading to a meeting make sure you know who's there. This is easy when it's just one-on-one, but can be slightly trickier if you're going to an event, although most event organisers will send out a list of attendees the day before. This is the chance to take the upper hand, know their names and where they are from, know who you want to talk to and who you want to avoid. I have a great strategy to help you do this, but I'll get to that later. A top tip for attending face-to-face meetings is to ask who else will be present, as this will give you the opportunity to research them on LinkedIn and their website.

When? Don't be late – this is some of the best advice I can give you. We all see those people who walk in halfway through a meeting and immediately have a negative view. Know the time and date and try to be early. Someone like a Red will be particularly impatient, and if you're late there's a good chance you have destroyed any chance you had of making the sale. Being late shows disrespect and that you value your time more than theirs.

Where? This is a biggie – always know where you're going. Going back to the previous point, most people are late because they didn't know where they are going. You can avoid this by looking up the location beforehand, checking the directions and planning what time you need to leave to ensure you arrive on time, if not early. With the help of our friend, Google, this shouldn't be a hard task. I have been in situations where I am on my way to a networking meeting and can't find my way, and it makes me anxious and stressed. I know I'm not the only one that feels like this, and you can avoid it by being prepared.

When travelling to a new place it's always a good idea to ask your prospective customer about traffic and parking and say something like, "As I have never been to that area before, allow me five minutes leeway in case the traffic is bad".

What? The final part of being prepared is knowing what you need. For example, do you need business cards, a laptop, or marketing materials? One of my biggest pet hates is when I phone someone ready to hand over my money, and have my card in my hand ready to give them the all-important details to make that sale. Then they turn around and say, "Sorry, give me a minute whilst I try to find a pen", then I have to hang on the line while they run around like a headless chicken looking for a pen. Now they're wasting my time and I wish I had never called in the first place, but then again I am high Red.

The process is not industry specific and there will be things that you know you need to do in your role, but the key is to make sure they are done and you are as prepared as you can be. Sometimes you'll have to think on your feet for sure, but people can tell when you are blagging and it may work on occasion but it won't work indefinitely. This is one reason I am a big fan of the checklist.

Checklists

There is a great book by Matthew Syed called *Black Box Thinking*, subtitled 'Marginal gains and the secrets of high performance'. He analyses the success of the airline industry in minimising accidents. There are now fewer airline accidents than at any other time in history and you now have more chance of winning the lottery than of dying in a plane accident. He identifies that the airline industry must look back and learn from mistakes, correct them and work them into the process for the future. One of the key ways they do this is with simple, yet comprehensive, checklists.

So, if they work for airline pilots and doctors (and they do), they will work for something as simple as sales.

It's a good idea to create a checklist for sales meetings. You could use an online tool like Trello, Google Keep, or Evernote. You could just type it up, print it out and stick it on the wall.

Whatever method you choose there are three areas you need to cover:

1. **Background**

    1. What do you know about the customer?

    2. What's the history – have you called them before?

    3. Are they a current client?

    4. What have they bought from you before?

2. **Equipment**

    1. What do you need to take with you or have to hand?

    2. Do you have a pen and paper?

    3. Have you charged your phone/laptop?

4. Have you got Wi-Fi access?

5. Do you have anything to demonstrate to the client?

3. Purpose

1. Why are you meeting/calling?

2. What do you want to achieve from the meeting?

3. What's in it for them? (This is the most important bit!)

To reiterate my point, be prepared. It's not that hard, it doesn't take that much time and it can make or break the sale.

Step 2: Do Your Research

People buy people, it doesn't matter what way you make the sale – over the phone or in person. But before you make a sale you have to be organised and do some research.

The obvious question here is 'How much research?'

I worked with one team who couldn't figure out why their salesperson wasn't hitting their target. Back in the day when I was working in telesales, it was life before the internet, and the expectation was that we would be on the phone for 3-4 hours a day making between 70-100 calls. But, remember it's about quality not quantity. In today's world, we have tools that help us research and therefore this can take a little more time. When I reviewed my client's call time, I found in an 8-hour day only 35 minutes was spent on the phone. This wasn't because he was lazy, but because he was doing so much research that he wasn't left with much time to make the phone calls. Or even more frustrating, he would do the research and then when it came to making the call the person he wanted to speak to wasn't available.

Do some quick research, and find out the rest by talking to people. That is one of the great things about being in sales; you get to find out all kinds of things about people's businesses. And as we know, information is power, but more on this later.

It's at this point you want to find out who you should be talking to, who is the M.A.N. Doing your research will help ensure you are talking to the right person and not wasting your time. Once you have the name of the decision maker, write it down in your 'CRM system', database, diary... whatever it is that you use to keep track of your leads. Get the email address, phone number and whatever else you can... if you can't get the email address can you guess it by looking at the format of the other email addresses in the organisation? For example, if the contact email listed on the website is info@abccompany.co.uk, then if the MD is called John his email could potentially be John@abccompany.co.uk.

A CRM is a Customer Relationship Management system and quite frankly a godsend. It's a documentation device that will record all the data you build on your current and potential clients. The CRM system can record that you spoke to so-and-so on such a date and they would like to be called back in six months' time. It is a more efficient and cleaner way of managing what would have been your diary of old. It's also a great place to store information on things that help to build rapport – children's names, favourite football team, last holiday destinations, etc – Yellows and Greens especially love this as it makes your call so much more personal.

Back to your research. There are several things you should look into before meeting a potential client. Find out what their company does, and what their products and services are. Research into their competitors, who they are and what makes your potential client different. Conduct research into their industry. For example, find out what others in the industry do around sales, what the average return and average sales value is for that industry. If you are in marketing you might want to know what the average email open rate is for someone in that industry.

Step 3: How Do You Introduce Yourself?

In business, you will speak to new people all the time. It's important you know how to introduce yourself properly. Most people think they know how to do this, but make the common mistake of rabbiting on and lose the listener's engagement. Don't worry, we all make this mistake to begin with, as it can be easy to get carried away talking about something when you're passionate.

A formula I use when introducing myself is one I like to call the W-Introduction because it's a winning introduction. It goes like this:

> *'Hi, I'm Alison Edgar, The Entrepreneur's Godmother and Managing Director of Sales Coaching Solutions. What we do is work with startups, micros, owner-managed businesses and sales teams, to teach them how to sell more of their fantastic products and services. What we teach is our Four Key Pillars of Sales Methodology; we do this through a variety of workshops, online courses and 1-1 coaching packages. How this helps you is that it gives you the skills and knowledge to make more money and ultimately grow your business."*

The W-Introduction can be broken up into four parts which makes it easier to remember when delivering:

1. Who are you?

2. Where are you from?

3. What do you do?

4. What's in it for them?

The mistake most people make is by stopping after the third W. They will say something like:

"Hi, I'm Jane from Cake World and we make custom cakes for all types of occasions, including weddings, christenings and birthdays."

It's the fourth W that engages the listener, because up until that fourth W all you've done is spoken about yourself but they want to know what you can do for them. It's never about you, it's always about them. When I teach this on my workshop I usually ask everyone what they would do if they were on the *Titanic* – if they had left all their friends, family, pets at home, who would they want to save when the ship starts sinking. Who would you want to save? The answer for most people is 'me'. If you're on the *Titanic* with no close friends and family you most likely want to save yourself. It's the same in business, everyone is in it for themselves, whether it's to build their network, increase brand awareness or find new leads.

You only get one chance to make a first impression; do not leave it to chance. Get it right every time. That fourth W makes what you're saying so much more interesting, for example:

"Hi, my name is Jane. I am the Managing Director of the award-winning Cake World. We make custom cakes for all occasions, including weddings, christenings and birthdays. From shape, colour, flavour and theme, we can make you the cake of your dreams. After 10 years of marriage, statistics show that most brides remember more about their wedding cake than they do about their guests. Cakes are a key focal point for celebrations and we create unforgettable cakes which are unique to you and your special day."

It is the emotion in the fourth W, the 'what is in it for them', that sticks.

Setting the Table

When attending a sales meeting or speaking on a sales call, it's important that you set the table. By this I mean lay out the agenda for what is going to happen. When you go to a restaurant and see two knives, two forks and a spoon on the table, you know you're having three courses. On a sales call, you need to set the table so there are no surprises. For example, "First I want to find out more about you and what your needs are, then I will explain what we can offer, the benefits of this, and look at how we can move forward." If you try to make the sale and the customer isn't expecting it, it will only backfire. It is also a good idea to mention how long the meeting or call will take and ask the customer if this fits in with their timeframe which is particularly important on the phone.

If you're a Red you will have no issues leading the meeting. For Greens and Blues, this technique will help you take charge and lead the dance.

Step 4: Questioning Techniques

I am evangelical about questioning techniques: in my opinion this is the most important part of everything I teach. When you get this right, it can lead to great things.

Once you have introduced yourself to a potential customer and established a connection, you need to understand their needs, and to do this you need to ask the right questions. The customer might not know what they need, but you need to work with them to discover it.

When I teach this part in my workshops, I ask, "Who has young children?" and a few hands will go up, then I say, "Who was a child?" and this always gets 100% of hands in the air (I love getting 100%). So, let me ask you, "Were you a child once?" (Hopefully you answered yes, or something funny is going on.) When we are three-year-old children, our brains are like sponges trying to learn as much as we can, and the most common word you will hear come from a three-year-old's mouth is 'why'. Why this? Why that? Why? Why? Why? If you have been a parent with a three-year-old this will start to drive you a bit mad.

Between the ages of 0-3 adult to child ratios are usually low, either 1:1 or 2:1, because the child tends to be with the parents or grandparents and is the centre of attention. Therefore, when they ask a question they get an answer, so they continue to ask "Why?"

At the age four or five kids go to school, and in a class of approximately 30 children a teacher can't answer every "why?", so children are taught to be polite and put up their hands when they have a question. They go from being little sponges asking open questions to polite children asking closed questions like "Can I...? Please may I...?" When you're at the stage of finding out needs, you need to break the habit of a lifetime and revert back to your three-year-old self.

The four most common types of questions are: open, closed, leading and rhetorical. The most important of these are the open questions.

This is one of the most powerful things I can teach you, and if you take anything from this book, let it be this.

- **Open questions** – Are those that start with who, what, when, where, why and how. They cannot be answered with one-word answers, which is why they are crucial at this point of discovery.

- **Closed questions** – These are ones that are answered with yes or no. They are great for getting confirmation of understanding but don't necessarily tell you anything about the customer.

- **Leading questions** – This is when you put the answer in the question in order to get the response you want.

- **Rhetorical questions** – These are questions that are asked to create a dramatic effect rather than to get an answer.

Here are some great open questions to ask at this stage:

- What is it that your company does?

- How long have you been doing that?

- How many people are in your company?

- What are the biggest challenges you face in your company?

- Who's in charge of …?

- When are you hoping to do that?

- Who else are you considering for the job?

- Where are you based?

- Who are your customers?

These questions will give you so much information about your potential customer and will help you discover what they really need and if you can help them. You can use open questions in all aspects of your life, not just sales, which is why I'm evangelical about them as they can quite literally change your life. People think I'm lucky, but I am just a thorough believer in open questions, and if you don't ask, you don't get.

When Neil and I got married we chose to tie the knot in Jamaica; we got married without any family and friends but arranged a Caribbean themed wedding reception in Clydebank for when we got back home. We had a steel band and fluorescent palm trees which we acquired from the Dorothy Perkins display window (another great example of open questions). Everything was planned; it was going to be pure dead brilliant. And it was... apparently.

Unfortunately, due to technical difficulties, our flight was delayed and we were stuck in the brace position instead of partying with our family and friends. It was one of the most upsetting days of my life.

When we got home I phoned British Airways and asked to be put through to the CEO's office. I was amazed I got through.

I spoke to the CEO's PA and instead of getting mad I used my questioning skills, "How do you think that feels?" "What should I tell my family?" I kept completely calm – if you remember the colours,

I was being Green rather than Red. The poor PA was so empathetic and upset for me, she was nearly in tears, and a couple of hours later she phoned back to say we could have some free tickets.

I used my questioning skills again. First I asked, "Where are the tickets for?" "Anywhere in the world", she replied. Great I thought, Australia here I come. Next, I asked, "When?" "Anytime" she replied. Then it was "How many?" "Well, two", she said. "But what about my Mum and Dad? And Neil's Mum and Dad?" "Ok, six tickets then." "What type of tickets are these?" Yes, you guessed it... she upgraded us to business class.

So, from the huge disappointment of missing my own wedding reception, I managed to get a holiday for six of us in Australia over Christmas and New Year, flying business class. It was the holiday of a lifetime and is one of the best examples of 'don't ask, don't get' I can give.

Step 5: Listen Up!

Listen up. I cannot say this enough: if you are going to go to the effort of asking the open questions and building a relationship with the potential customers, make sure you are listening. So many times I have been speaking to someone and think they are listening to me because they are asking me all these questions, only to realise that they are not actually listening when they ask me something I told them 10 minutes ago.

It's also a really good idea to capture as much of this data in your CRM. If you can't make notes in the meeting, write down as much as you can remember as soon it finishes.

One of my clients is a Yellow and sells a high-tech product to Blues, and he knows that when he has client meetings he will be overloaded with information. So that he doesn't forget any important details, he uses his phone to record the meeting. Beware, if you want to do this you must ask permission first. My client says this, "I know we'll speak about a lot of technical things which I would like to take back to my team and research, so how would you feel if I record the conversation?" Blues quite like this as it shows you are willing to do further research.

It's the little gems of information you find out during the open questions sessions that will lead you to the wow customer moments.

Wow moments are when you go above and beyond for your customer. If they say, "Yes, I would love to go ahead with this but I'm going away to France for two weeks so would prefer to wait until I get back", you could send them a pocket guide to France with a note wishing them a good time. It's moments like this customers don't expect and confirm their decision to work with you over someone else. It's also what keeps customers coming back after the first order.

If you're not actively listening you won't pick up on cues and it's likely that when they do eventually outline their needs you will have missed them and missed your opportunity.

I talk a lot but I am a big believer in shutting up and listening. This is like unpeeling an onion, actively listening to what the customer is saying. There are some salespeople that don't listen, they are just waiting until it is their turn to speak. They are focused only on making the sale, and nothing else matters.

Listening, understanding and respecting your customers can only lead to a better business relationship which will lead to more sales. Sometimes, whilst making a sale, you can be laying the foundation for the next sale and the next sale.

My top tip is: you have two ears and one mouth, and use them in that order.

Step 6: Get the Need

So, you've put in the work and you've asked the open questions to help you uncover what it really is that your potential customer needs.

But how do you meet that need? It's all very well knowing it but now you have to do something about it.

This is when you begin to sell your product or service. Up until this point you shouldn't have done too much talking about yourself, and a good rule to remember is 80:20, the customer talks 80% of the time and you the other 20%.

Before you start reeling off the company catalogue, think – are you selling too soon?

This is one of the biggest mistakes I see salespeople make. They start selling their product or service before they even know what it is the customer needs. This is probably a good time to specify the difference between a want and a need. A customer may want a Ferrari but what they actually need is a Nissan Qashqai. If you ask Jon what car he wants, he will tell you the car of his dreams, but if you play detective and use open questions, you'll find Jon has three kids and likes to take his dog for a walk in the countryside at the weekend. Therefore, the Ferrari of Jon's dreams isn't actually what he needs.

If you have done your research and spent time getting to know your potential customer, you should have a pretty good idea of what their needs are. If you feel you still don't know what they need, then revisit your questioning techniques and ask more open questions.

Sometimes you will get to this point and find there is no need for your service. When this happens, don't try and force your products or services on someone who isn't interested, as there is nothing more infuriating than a pushy salesperson. It is a waste of energy, and you might be talking yourself out of a nice easy sale that would have come sometime in the future.

Now you've got the need, it's time to summarise and commit. This is when those closed questions come into play. The reason that we use closed questions at this stage is to ensure that both parties are on the same page. This is where we summarise what they have said to confirm our understanding of their needs; getting a 'yes' commitment at this stage puts them in the 'yes' mindset.

Let me illustrate what I mean with this example of a customer looking for some help with their website:

> *'Ok, Mr Customer, just to make sure I've understood what you have said –*

1. You are looking to have a website that better reflects your brand?

2. You want to increase website traffic?

3. You want to increase the average time spent on your website?

If after these questions you are not on the same page, you need to go back to your open questions and find out where you went wrong.

Step 7: Features Tell, Benefits Sell

Before I tell you how to use this technique to help you close, you need to know the difference between features, needs and benefits:

- Feature – Something which defines your product or service

- Need – A customer requirement

- Benefit – A feature which satisfies the need

Once you've established your customer's needs, all you have to do is match your offer to the need. If only one of your products can solve their needs, then start with that. They don't need to know about your whole range if it isn't of any use to them.

If you're trying to sell someone your web design service, telling them it will be branded and mobile friendly isn't going to get you the sale. You need to sell benefits of these features:

"The benefit of using our web design service is that we can use your personal branding on every page, ensuring content and photos are in keeping with your brand values. Not only will this ensure a brand representative website, but it will ensure your target audience can relate to the page content, showing you understand their specific needs.

You want to increase traffic and the average time spent on your website. We know that 60% of your target market access the internet via their phones and tablets, so being mobile friendly will make it easier for your customers to find you, Google is likely to rank your website higher if it is mobile friendly. A mobile-friendly website makes it easier for users to navigate and use when on a mobile phone, which means your customers will stay on the website for longer, increasing the average visit time. Ultimately the longer they are on the website, the more they will know about your business and more likely will be to buy."

The important thing is to match the benefits of your services to their needs. If they said they are struggling with brand recognition, point out how your product or service can help with this. So many people just list features and not what the features can do for the customer.

Remember to clearly link and illustrate this for your customer so they can see in their minds exactly what extra value you are adding to their company, and how they will recoup their investment in your service.

At this point, I would like you to reflect on how you may have approached sales in the past. Can you see where you may have missed out on sales because you didn't know or follow the process?

I call this the Successful Sales Process, but it can be easy to get it wrong and miss a step. You are going to have to approach things in a different manner and that will take time and practice.

Listing the places where you need to focus can help you tackle those issues. In changing any type of behaviour pattern, we first need to recognise the behaviour we have been manifesting. This isn't meant to be a deep, sit-on-the-couch psychology session, but it is just how we all learn! And if helps you hit your sales targets then it will all be worth it!

Step 8: Asking for the Order

When I run sales training sessions, at the start I ask everyone to write down their goals on what they want to learn. Approximately 70% of the room will say they want to learn to close sales. When I hear this I do a mini fist pump to myself because I already know that the reason they can't close is because they haven't opened. They haven't followed the process, so didn't get the need, and therefore have sold too soon or didn't have the confidence to ask for the order. Usually, before I even get to this point, I will see the light bulb moments when they realise they couldn't close because they never opened.

The majority of the time, the customer will tell you when they want to buy, by giving you subliminal messages and asking questions. Most people miss the signals, especially the Greens and Blues. The Greens run at a slower pace and don't always recognise early buying signals, and the Blues can get carried away with the detail so that when the customer gives them the signal they ignore it because they want to continue talking about the features and benefits. An example of typical buying signals is head nodding, leaning in, speaking about the future and asking open questions. When the customer wants to buy, the roles reverse, and the customer is the one asking open questions such as, "What discount is available?", "When would it be ready by?" and "What colour would we have it in?". Yellows can sometimes be the easiest colour to sell to because they will openly admit they want something. In fact I have seen a Yellow jump up and down with excitement at the prospect of buying (I may be guilty of this too). You would think at this point the salesperson would go for the close, but they don't usually because they aren't listening, reiterating my earlier point of the importance of actively listening to your customers.

Going back to 'old skool' sales, a common phrase that would fly about the office was "ABC – always be closing". I think in the 21st century this comes over as a little pushy and is something a Red salesperson is often guilty of. A Red customer might like this fast-action sales approach, but for a Green it might come across as intimidating. But as I said, this is the 21st century and there is more than one approach to closing a sale.

I like to keep things simple and work around the principle of 'taking an order', like you would in a restaurant or shop. There are a couple of ways you can go about doing this.

The assumptive close

This is my favourite way to close because it's quick and to the point, an example of an assumptive close would be "When would you like to start?". This sounds incredibly presumptive, but if you have asked all the right questions and built up enough rapport with the client, you should be adept enough to spot the signs and know that the sale is made. The trick is to pick up on the early buying signals, and as soon as you spot them you need to go in for the close. You need confidence when closing, but even more so when taking the assumptive approach, I walk into every sale knowing that I have it. I never doubt myself – after all what's the worst that can happen? They could say no, but that's it. For me the assumptive close is instinctive, and the best advice I can give you when taking this approach is to be like Nike and "Just Do It".

The alternative close

This is the process of asking for an order by providing the customers with two options. This can be an effective approach when dealing with a Green who struggles to make decisions and might find the assumptive close too forward. An example of an alternative close is, "When would you like to start, Monday or Tuesday?". Again, this can be a bit presumptive, but if you followed the process it should work perfectly. Going back to the questioning techniques, this is when the leading questions come into play, as you are giving the customer the answer you want. Only ever give two options, as too many choices can be an overload and will confuse the customer.

The best-case, worst-case scenario

This works particularly well for someone like a Green who can often be worried about taking risks and investing in new products or services. This is where you can use the Netflix approach, where you offer a free trial or special offer before they invest on a long-term basis; for example, "Worst-case scenario, you take us up on the free trial and don't get on with the product, best-case scenario, you absolutely love it and continue to use it after the trial". It's a bit like a try-before-you-buy, and if they dislike it then it's no harm no foul, as it didn't cost them anything in the first place. Another example of this is the "no win, no fee" model used by personal injury lawyers.

'The fear close'

This is a classic and should be used in genuine cases as customers will soon see through you if you are trying to pull a fast one. A typical fear close will sound like this: "Buy before midnight and receive 25% off", or "Quick, only 5 tickets left, book yours now". The purpose of the fear close is to generate fear, not startling crippling fear, but the fear of missing out (FOMO). Adding a deadline rushes the customer's decision, forcing them to choose there and then whether to buy or not, and if the customer is a typical Yellow who doesn't like to be left out, they will probably buy.

However, you have to be careful with this approach. One, because if it becomes apparent to your customers that you put on a 'last-minute deal' every other Thursday, they will just wait until then to buy and only ever purchase something from you when it's discounted. Two, speeding up someone's decision to buy can lead to buyer's remorse.

Ladies, you will know what I mean by this: it's like that time you bought those black ankle boots you didn't really need but there was 25% off for a limited time only, yet you never wear them because you have two other pairs exactly the same and you wish you had never bought them. After the customer has bought the on-sale item or service, they will think about it clearly and realise they never really wanted it and will usually try and return the item or cancel the appointment, resulting in both you and the customer having a negative experience.

The fear close can be great for driving last-minute sales, but beware of the potential backlash and only use it when it's a genuine offer.

Customers are savvy and know when you're spinning them a line or lying. If you try and fear close by saying, "This is your last chance to buy before the price goes up" and a week later the price is still the same, you will lose the trust of your customers and it will have a negative impact on your credibility and reputation. Sales is all about a win-win situation; if you're lying at this point the relationship is never going to work, since a strong customer relationship is the foundation of every sale.

One of the best tips I can give you when it comes to closing a sale is to keep schtum. One of the biggest mistakes people make when selling is asking for the order then continuing to speak before the customer even has a chance to think.

When it comes to closing, the first one to speak loses. Customers will need time to think about an offer before making any decision. This can often lead to an awkward silence, but just hold your nerve and don't speak. It's at this point the salesperson will start to feel uncomfortable and start throwing deals and special offers on the table. This is a huge mistake. Don't give away something you don't have to. Wait for the customer to speak and then, once you know their thoughts, you can start negotiating.

Everyone processes things differently and some need more time than others before deciding. Don't rush the process, go at the pace of the customer.

This really is one of the best pieces of advice I can give you to help you close a sale. Sometimes silence can be more powerful than words.

Step 9: Objections

> *"A no is not forever, just for now"*
> – Will King, Founder of King of Shaves

It would be great if everyone always said yes! But they don't... I may be good, but nobody can stop every objection.

We all get objections, but we don't all handle them as well as we could. Sometimes we take them personally, sometimes we're offended by them. Don't be – it's all part of the process.

Sales is a bit like dating – an objection in sales is like a knock-back in dating. If someone doesn't want to go on a date with you, very rarely would they say, "I can't meet you because I don't like you", instead they will let you down gently and say, "I'm sorry, I'm washing my hair that night". They don't want to give you the full story. It's your job to detect whether they really are washing their hair or they are just not that interested, and it's the same in sales.

In the world of business we call these true and false objections. A true objection is when someone is telling the truth and has no need for your product or service at this time. But as my friend, Will King, says, "A no is not forever, just for now", and just because they don't need what you're offering right now, it doesn't mean they won't need it in the future. A false objection is just an excuse for not buying or a fob-off because someone doesn't know how to tell you they are not interested – it's the dating scenario again. The most common objections are:

- **Need** – What you're offering doesn't fit the customer's needs.

- **Time** – The customer doesn't have time or it isn't the right time for them to purchase.

- **Alternative source** – The customer is already using your competitor.

- **Bad experience** – The customer previously had a negative experience from similar products or services in your industry.

- **Cost** – The customer doesn't have the budget or your competitor is cheaper.

If you have followed the process and used open questions to get the need, when it comes to the close, the customer shouldn't object. An objection is a sign that you're selling too soon. The process is a circle because you just keep going round until you convert the sale, but when someone objects you go back to asking the open questions and use them to work out if the objection is true or false.

Overcoming Objections

Here are seven simple steps to overcoming any objection:

1. Listen – don't jump in before they have finished explaining

2. Questions – always use open questions and be empathetic

3. Reassure and commit

4. Answer with relevant benefits

5. Confirm and close

6. Negotiate

7. Summarise and commit

Does this look familiar to you? That's right, these steps are literally the stages of the sales process.

I want to break down each of the objections listed above and explain how you can overcome the common objections that you are more than likely to come up against when selling.

Objection 1 – Need

The first common objection is need, when the customer claims to have no need for the product or service you're offering. This can be a true or false objection – you can't sell to everyone, and not everyone needs what you're selling. When it's a false objection it's usually because the customer does not understand what it is you're trying to sell.

If you're a vegetarian and someone knocks on your door to sell you a ticket to the local cider and sausage festival, there's a good chance you're going to decline their offer. If the vegetarian said, "No thank you, I'm a vegetarian so a sausage festival doesn't appeal to me", this is a true objection as the offer doesn't fit the needs of the customer. The salesperson has failed to ask the qualifying question "Do you eat meat?" before selling, and therefore has fallen into the trap of selling too soon.

What does a false objection look like? If you're selling Google AdWords to a hotel and they say, "No thank you, our guests find us organically and book straight through our website", this could be a true or false objection. If they were at full occupancy for the next two years, it is understandable that they don't feel the need to invest in advertising. But if they are at 50% occupancy then why wouldn't they want to fill the rest of their rooms and maximise revenue. The customer has given the false objection because they don't clearly understand the benefits of Google AdWords and what it can do for their business. The salesperson has failed to identify the needs of the customer and match up the relevant benefits. Once the salesperson has used open questions to detect the need, they could say, "It's great that your customers go direct to your website, but you're currently ranked on the second page of Google. If you invested in Google AdWords you could increase enquiries by reaching the unknown market."

Also, remember what Will King said. If the hotel is telling you the truth and they are at maximum occupancy for the next two years, then they clearly don't need you now. But that doesn't mean they won't need you in a year or two when they are trying to fill rooms again.

Objection 2 – Time

Time is another common objection you will hear when trying to sell. A time objection can come in many forms, such as they don't have time right now or it's not the right time in the business. The examples below show how you can overcome time objections, but also how important it is to understand the context of the objection.

I often run sales workshops, and when my team are out networking speaking to prospective clients, one of the common objections they hear is, "Oh, it sounds great, but I can't make that day". Now, is the customer telling the truth or are they just trying to fob us off? One way to overcome this is always to have additional dates set, so that you can say, "That's no problem, we are running another workshop in January." If it was a true objection they should go ahead and book the next available date, but if it's a false objection and they really don't want to come, they will make another excuse. You can take this approach whether you're a product- or service-based industry, as all you are really doing is offering them an alternative that might better suit their needs.

Another common time objection is when people say, "I don't have the time to talk right now, sorry". This is one you will usually receive over the phone. An easy way to overcome this is to ask when they're available by saying, "No problem, when are you next available to talk? I will give you a call when you have more time". Reschedule another date to call them back, and if they are telling the truth they will have no problem re-scheduling and usually be specific about when to call them back. If it's a false objection and they are fobbing you off, they will faff around before giving you a vague time like "Call me in about an hour". Someone who gives you a false objection will also try and dodge your call when you call back, but that doesn't mean you shouldn't bother. After all, are they objecting to the idea of a sales call or what you have to offer?

I know I'm repeating this, but it really is true that just because someone doesn't need you now it doesn't mean they won't need you in the future. For example, if you're a furniture provider and meet someone who is opening a new café in a year and they say, "We aren't currently looking for furniture", that is a true objection, they don't need it now but they will in a year's time, if not before. You don't want to let this potential customer slip away, so what you can do is schedule a date to continue your discussion closer to the time and they will be more than happy to do this.

It's imperative that you are able to recognise when someone is objecting but genuinely interested. My Mum, who passed away a few years ago, loved going to the races, so every year as a family tradition my sister and I organised a trip to Newbury races. It was my turn to organise the trip and book the tickets, but as you can probably guess, I'm a pretty busy lady. When the man from Newbury Racecourse called me to see if I wanted to book tickets (we've become regulars) I said, "I'm just about to head into a meeting. Can you give me a call back in an hour?", a true objection as I was genuinely heading into a meeting. When he called back, I said, "Yes, I do want to book tickets, but I'm driving so can you call me back tomorrow". Again another true objection. When he called back the third time, I said, "I really do want to book tickets but I'm just about to go on another call, please can you call me back tomorrow after five". This was another true objection. I really did want to book tickets, but I am hard to pin down. In the end the man from Newbury Racecourse had to phone me 12 times before I finally booked tickets. THAT'S 12 TIMES! It's important that when someone is genuinely interested in what you're selling but gives a true objection like I did, you are persistent and patient. It will pay off in the end.

Objection 3 – Alternative Source

An alternative source objection is centred around your competitors and can come in two forms. One, the customer has already bought from your competitor, or two, they are in the process of buying and comparing you and your competitor to find the best deal. Here's how you can gain a positive outcome from both situations.

There will come a time when you meet someone who is your ideal customer and you know your product or service is perfect for them. This has happened to me on more than one occasion. I am asking open questions and can tell they are a perfect fit for what I have to offer. Then they tell me they recently invested in a sales training course with a competitor. At this point you want to bang your head on a wall as you are frustrated you have just wasted your time. Stop. Perseverance is key. If you walk away now then you really would have wasted your time. Put your detective hat on and use your open questions. Here are some great questions I ask that you can tailor to your business:

- How did you find the initial training?

- How have you implemented the training in your business?

- What results have you experienced in your business since attending the training?

- What was it that encouraged you to work with that particular trainer?

- What are your plans heading into the future?

These questions give me so much information and the potential to turn this objection into a sale. If the customer is struggling to implement the training they learned, I offer my services as a way of complementing what they have already learned. Always point out how your product or service complements that of the competitors and how they can work with both of you to maximise results. Never, and I mean never, talk badly about the opposition, it will only lead to a negative view of you. Business is about collaboration, and if you respect your competition they will respect you.

Another situation where a potential customer will use one of your competitors as an objection is when they are in the decision-making process of who to buy from. For example, if two electronic retailers both sell the exact same laptop, why should a customer buy from one over the other? If retailer 1 is slightly cheaper than retailer 2 then the customer's decision is easy, right? When you can't compromise on price it's all about the added values. Retailer 1 might be £10 cheaper but retailer 2 is willing to offer you a year's free warranty, complimentary anti-virus software and a year's subscription to Microsoft. Even though retailer 1 is cheaper, the customer will buy from retailer 2 because the added valued outweighs the cost saving.

Objection 4 – Bad experience

This one is quite self-explanatory. It's when a customer has had a negative experience within your industry before and therefore objects when you go in for the close.

A good example of this is when a new restaurant opens. I'm going to run through a dialogue between a customer and business owner to demonstrate how you can overcome this type of objection. To set the scene, a proud owner of a new sushi restaurant is handing out flyers in a busy town centre to generate custom.

Restaurant owner: Good afternoon sir, I'm the proud owner of the new sushi restaurant on the corner. We serve the finest hand-made sushi, made fresh to order, it has a wonderful atmosphere and we can cater to parties for all occasions and sizes.

Customer: No thank you, I refuse to eat sushi after it made me rather ill a few years back.

Restaurant owner: I'm sorry, that sounds terrible. Where did you buy the sushi from?

Customer: It was one of the pre-packed sushi things from a supermarket. I couldn't go to work for two days after.

Restaurant owner: Food poisoning can be horrible, so I understand how this bad experience could lead to a dislike of sushi. Was that the first time you ate sushi?

Customer: No, I loved sushi before that, but now I just can't take the risk.

Restaurant owner: That's such a shame. Have you ever tried freshly prepared sushi?

Customer: No, I haven't.

Restaurant owner: It's very nice. At my restaurant, we hand-make all sushi to order and only use the freshest fish. As a restaurant, we adhere to strict health and safety regulations to ensure all our food is delicious and safe to eat. I would love to be the person to change your mind about sushi.

Customer: Oh, I don't know.

Restaurant owner: Why don't you and your family come in on Friday and have dinner with us? I will reserve a table especially for you and I'll even show you how we make the sushi.

Customer: Wow, that would be fantastic. My children would love it.

Restaurant owner: Lovely, it will be great. We could do 6pm or 6:30pm on Friday – how does that sound?

Customer: 6pm sounds brilliant. I will let my wife know we have dinner plans.

Restaurant owner: Excellent, I'll see you Friday at 6. I look forward to meeting your family. Have a great day.

Customer: See you then.

Can you see how following the process can enable you to overcome the objection? The restaurant owner listened to the objection and was empathetic, and this is particularly important when dealing with a Green. He then used open questions to get the full story and reassure the customer by explaining the features and benefits of eating at his restaurant. This can easily be applied to your own business. Another way to overcome this, especially in the service industry, is offer a free taster. I will often give potential customers a free consultation before they commit to anything long term. That way they can get a feel for how I work and see that this experience will be different from their previous negative one.

Objection 5 – Cost

The final objection I want to go through with you is cost. This one is a bit of a beast. It is probably the most common objection you will hear throughout your entire career.

When you're trying to sell a product or a service to someone, particularly in B2B sales, the customer will say, "We don't have the budget". Well, I will let you into a little secret – you can always find money for something you really want. This means that either they were never interested in the first place and you failed to detect this at the early stages of the sales process, or they are trying to get a cheaper price. A really great tip here, especially for those in B2B sales, is to understand how budgets work across different industries. There are peak times for selling to every industry and this usually coincides with when they need to spend their budget.

When someone says "We don't have a budget", the best question that you can ask them is, "What is your budget?" You could argue that this question should have been asked earlier in the sales process when you were 'getting the need', but the fact is most people won't tell you their budget that early on.

This is where we need to negotiate.

This is one of my favourite subjects, I think probably because this is really at the heart of business. It is the nitty-gritty of the actual transaction between customer and business. And strangely enough, given its importance, it is one of the areas that salespeople and business owners alike most like to avoid.

I negotiate on everything, except at Tesco's where I think I might get a few funny looks from the customer checkout people! Why wouldn't you negotiate? Saving money is as good as making money if you are an entrepreneur or someone who has been working hard all day to earn your cash.

There are two sides to every negotiation, the customer's and the seller's. You will experience both, so I'm going to show you how to deal with both. I'll start with negotiating as the seller to help you overcome cost objections.

The key to negotiating is knowing your numbers. Know the value of your product and service and know the cost. For those of you who don't know the difference, cost is how much it takes you to produce the product or deliver the service, value is what it brings to the customer. The sales training I provide is invaluable because the skills I teach my clients can quite literally earn them millions.

Here's what you need to know:

- What is your price point?

- Where do you break even?

- What is your cost of sale?

The bottom line is to know what things cost. When I worked in hotels it was about calculating room occupancy and the average room rate. If a marketing consultant wanted to know how much it costs just to open their doors, this would include time, travel, and overheads.

Also, you need to know what your margin is. 'The rule of thirds' is a good baseline and a rule I have used since day one. This is how it works:

- 1/3 – What does it cost to deliver your product or service?

- 1/3 – What do you need to pay yourself? You need a minimum income to keep you going. How much do you need each month?

- 1/3 – What should you be saving or re-investing? You need money to grow the business and a slush fund to keep you afloat.

For example, if you produce a box of cakes, the first third is the cost of the ingredients, packaging and overheads. If this comes to £4 then you would sell the cakes to your customers for £12. The first £4 ensures you break even, the second £4 is what you pay yourself for your time and the last £4 is what you re-invest back into the company.

There are lots of pricing strategies you can use, but this is a simple one that has always worked for me.

A top tip for negotiating: start high and let them knock you down. You can always negotiate down, but you can never negotiate up.

The ideal situation is to not negotiate on price but give some 'added value', preferably not added time, but increased volume. As in the previous example of the two retailers selling the same laptop, if you can offer an extra thing so that both customer and salesperson feel they have a win-win situation, then this is perfect.

If you feel that someone is screwing you down on price, then you won't be happy. You might not deliver the customer service to the best of your abilities, and the relationship may be doomed to fail. But if you can get the best price and the best deal then you are building a long-term relationship which will be fruitful for both sides.

Sometimes in negotiating you have to be ballsy, for fortune favours the brave. But this confidence will only come from knowing your numbers.

Someone who is a great example of this is my pal, Jordan Daykin, CEO of GripIt Fixings who was the youngest person to receive funding on *Dragon's Den* at the age of 18. For those of you who haven't seen Jordan's pitch, Deborah Meaden made an offer to invest of £80,000 for 30% of the business. This was more than Jordan was willing to give away. A lot of entrepreneurs on *Dragon's Den* make the mistake of accepting the first offer instead of negotiating. Jordan knew his numbers and negotiated the 30% down to 25% and reached a win-win. That 5% that Deborah tried to negotiate is now worth £950,000. This is why you need to know your numbers. What doesn't seem like much now could be worth a lot in the future.

That's how you negotiate as the seller to overcome cost objections, but what about negotiating as the buyer? Asking for discount can sound abrupt, so instead I always ask for the 'best price'. Instead of starting high you want to start low. As the buyer, you want to let the salesperson drive the price up until you meet in the middle. A good salesperson would offer you added values, but as a savvy buyer you could suggest these added values in exchange for paying their desired price.

Remember when I missed my own wedding reception because mechanical breakdown delayed my flight? The outcome was a good negotiation, but I had a clear vision and I was confident enough to be able to negotiate my way up beyond my initial preconceptions of what I thought was possible. Always be prepared for this eventuality, as we often talk ourselves out of so much.

Testing intention

Before we move on to the next stage in the sales process I want to go over a technique called testing intention. When someone expresses interest in your business, but continues to object (a bit like I did with the man from Newbury Racecourse), you can test their intention to buy by asking a simple question. In this situation, I always say the same thing, "For my clarity and sanity, on a scale of 1-5 with 1 being not likely and 5 being highly likely, how likely are you to go ahead with this purchase?" Providing a scale makes it easier and more comfortable for the customer to turn you down. As I've mentioned before, Greens struggle to make decisions and because of their nature find it difficult to say no, especially if they think they are going to offend you. That's why this technique of testing intention can be really effective.

If after you've asked the question the customer gives you a 1 or a 2, you can go back in to objection handling and find out why they don't want to purchase. If they give you a 4 or a 5, this is a clear buying signal and you should go in for the close.

The great thing about testing intention is it separates the wheat from the chaff. It's OK for someone to say no, after all, you can't please all of the people all of the time. The earlier you can separate the wheat from the chaff, the better, as it's much better to get a no early on than six months down the line.

Step 10: Delivering to Expectations

Always deliver to expectations. If you say you're going to do something then make sure you do it. Remember my friends Jane and Mike who tried to do some PR work together? Well, one of the reasons that the relationship broke down and Jane lost the contract was because she couldn't deliver to expectations. She couldn't deliver what she had promised during the proposal.

My top tip is never over promise and under deliver. This will only ever reflect poorly on you. Some salespeople will do whatever they need to close the sale which looks great on their record but in the long run benefits no one.

Customer Journey

The sales process shows where you as the seller are in the sales process, but what about the customer? Sometimes the customer and the seller are on two different paths or at two different stages of the process, which is why when you try closing the customer might object. The customer journey shows where the customer is in their decision-making process in relation to the sales process.

When considering buying, the customer goes through eight stages:

1. I'm interested

2. Tell me more

3. You get me

4. I like what I'm hearing

5. We're a match

6. I want this

7. Wonder what it costs?

8. That works for me

Stage 1: I'm Interested

This is where you gain the interest of the customer using the strong W-Introduction formula. It's the fourth W, the 'what's in it for them?' that engages them and captures their interest.

Stage 2: Tell me more

This is when, as the seller, you are starting to ask open questions and conducting a bit of a fact find around the customer. You have retained their interest and they want to know more about what you can offer them. Someone who is interested will have lots to say, so if they start to really engage with your questions, take it as a positive.

Stage 3: You Get Me

Looking back at the sales process, this is when, as the seller, you should have understood their needs and used the summarise-and-commit techniques to confirm you know what they need. When you do this the customer is thinking "Yes, this person really understands me". The customer appreciates the fact you have listened and understood their needs.

Stage 4: I Like What I'm Hearing

As the seller, you would have matched the benefits of the product or service to the needs of the customer. At this point the customer is gaining knowledge around what you are trying to sell them and, if done correctly, should like what they hear.

Stage 5: We're a Match

Now the customer understands what you can offer them and how your product or service matches their needs, they can make a decision on whether you're the right choice for them. Providing you follow the sales process, they should see that you're a perfect match. Look out for buying signals at this stage.

Step 6: I Want This

Based on your recommendations and closing offer, the customer has developed a desire to buy. They like what you do and they want it.

Step 7: Wonder What It Costs?

This is when the objections start to evolve in the customer's mind. They like everything you have said and you almost have them, but committing to the purchase has them second-guessing themselves and justifying whether your product or service is what they really need and worth the cost.

Step 8: That Works for Me

After some objection handling and negotiation, you have reached a win-win offer. The customer recognises the value of your product or service and goes ahead with the purchase.

It's important you understand how the customer journey works in relation to the sales process. When both run parallel, the process is seamless. The problem occurs when the two don't run parallel and the customer and salesperson are in two different places. When this happens, the salesperson usually sells too soon and the customer objects because they don't fully understand what they are being sold.

Two Become One

"I genuinely believe when delivered correctly, sales and customer services are exactly the same thing." This is a statement I live by and let me tell you why. If what you're selling fulfils the customers' needs then it's not sales it's customer service you are delivering.

When I check into a hotel, my expectation is the receptionist will ask me my plans for my stay. By doing this they will uncover dinner in the restaurant and a massage in the spa would be right up my street. Yes, they are upselling their additional services, but at the same time providing me with a customer service. They have made my life easier. If you're a genuine fit for the customer and reach a win-win situation then it is a customer service.

That's why when I teach the customer service process it's the same as when I teach the sales process, because when delivered correctly they really are the same. In the words of the Spice Girls, "Two become one".

PILLAR THREE

STRATEGY

As I've mentioned throughout this book, sometimes it's difficult to work out where marketing finishes and sales begins, and if you did a poll of 100 salespeople and 100 marketeers the results would be completely different, but ultimately the most important thing is that they work together. Without their combined forces, like in my golf analogy, the ball will not go in the hole and the sale will not be made.

Whenever I know I have to travel to a new place I plan my journey. I work out my travel time and directions and the first thing I do when I get in my car is set my satnav. Very few of us when embarking on a new journey will just get in and drive. It's exactly the same with sales, you need to have a plan, a strategy that lays out where you want to go and what you want to achieve. After all, how do you know where to start if you don't know where you're going?

My Strategy

I know some of you, especially the Yellows and Greens, will want to know more about my personal journey. Like any journey, mine has a start, a route, vehicle, fuel, acceleration, a destination and of course a purpose. But on any well-planned journey there are traffic jams that hold us back.

The Start

Coming from a working-class family and being brought up in a high rise flat in Clydebank is something I have always been very proud of. My Mum and Dad, Alistair and Jessie, were incredibly hard working. Jessie would leave the house at 5am then again at 5pm every day to clean the local primary school, and as I've already said Alistair was a draughtsman on the shipyard, so from the start I was brought up knowing as strong work ethic was very important.

My affirmative years were spent at Clydebank High School. I loved school, hanging out with Angela McBain, Loraine Brown and the rest of my friends, and the school discos were always a huge highlight, dancing around my handbag to Simple Minds and Spandau Ballet. There was just one thing I didn't enjoy about school, and that was the lessons!! I was bright, but when it came to writing things down, that was tough, so I created coping strategies for what would now be known as dyslexia but at that time was mostly unrecognised.

In the mid 80s unemployment in Scotland was high and the benefits culture was rife. My parents were happy for me to leave school at 16 but not without a job, so without much searching I became a hotel receptionist at the Cameron House Hotel. I'm not talking about the salubrious one on the shores of Loch Lomond, I'm talking about the one at Hardgate Cross in Clydebank that had the nightclub at the top and the curry house at the bottom.

This stepping stone led me to managing hotels all over the world including Cape Town, Sydney, Ayres Rock and the Channel Islands for large brands like Radisson and Southern Suns. It was my responsibility to hit occupancy and yield targets, so I suppose this was where my first exposure to the importance of sales came from.

It was on my return to Scotland in the early 90s, a chance meeting at a party led to me meeting my husband Neil. As the relationship progressed my shift pattern and his Monday to Friday 9 to 5 job were becoming increasingly difficult to coordinate. It was time for me to find an alternative career when I saw an advert for a new BT Call Centre which was opening in Motherwell, and it seemed like a good time to discover if sales was for me. For years everyone had told me I could sell ice to the Eskimos, and it was time to put it to the test.

After an intensive three-week, sales and product knowledge training course at Kents Hill in Milton Keynes, 200 new recruits in the shiny call centre were ready to hit the phones, selling pagers (yip, people other than doctors actually bought them), early versions of mobile flip phones, mega streams and phone systems. The great thing about working for corporate companies is they are generous with their incentives, so when the announcement went out for a prize for the first person to make a sale on opening day, you can imagine how I was running up to ring the bell and put my result on the board. See, I told you I've always been one of the STARS.

A job change for Neil meant a move to Wiltshire in 1996. This led to me working in field sales for a well-known coffee company before embarking on a 15-year career as a top performer for an international media company, sprinkled with the birth of my two boys, Kieran and Connor, in 2000 and 2002. This gives a fast track view of my life – after all, this is a book about sales, not my autobiography.

The Why

My sales roles predominantly comprised of finding new customers and building relationships with small business owners to enable me to understand their needs and match the products we sold. In behaviours and process I have taught you what I did to become a top sales performer, so why did I choose to give it up to set up my own sales training company?

a. I had lost confidence in the products I was selling, the print directory market had declined with the rise of the internet, and as you know from the previous sections, product knowledge and belief is a key part of the sales process.

b. During my time in sales, the UK went through two recessions and it was hard for me to watch small businesses struggling because when the phone stopped ringing with new enquiries they did not know how to proactively sell their products or services.

As I've stated already, "Not on my watch". My passion and drive comes from knowing deep down I have a talent and skill which I can teach others which will improve their sales and change their fortunes. So that's exactly what I set out to do.

The Route

I started my business in 2011, but for a couple of years I didn't really take it seriously. Like Tom Daley, I jumped off the top diving board and took the plunge to start my own business, but like any learner I stalled a couple of times before I got on the road.

The real fun began in 2014 when I incorporated my business and found out about the Growth Vouchers programme. The project was the brainchild of Lord Young, the adviser to David Cameron and Margaret Thatcher. The Growth Vouchers programme was a multi-million pound government match funding scheme for small businesses to access specialist business advice in key areas such as recruitment, HR, marketing, sales and finance. For some unknown reason, the government had struggled to market the project and distribute the money.

So, what did I do? I used the Growth Vouchers programme to work with a number of clients, one of which was Marcus Whittington, the founder of Bath Boutique Stays, a holiday rental company of luxury houses and apartments in Bath. Over a series of sessions, I worked with Marcus and his team on their sales and customer service strategy. From the work we did together, Bath Boutique Stays' monthly turnover greatly increased, the following month they exceeded their sales target by £12,000, and ultimately quadrupled enquiries, tripled turnover and doubled profits.

At the time, Jane Austen's home was one of the luxury apartments in their portfolio. I knew that this, along with the excellent results they had experienced by working with me through the Growth Vouchers scheme, would make a great PR story. I did some research to find out who the M.A.N. was on the Growth Vouchers scheme and picked up the phone. It took a while but eventually I got through to someone on the scheme and pitched my idea to use Marcus as a case study. After a lot of follow-up and nagging on my part, I finally got the call to say they wanted to use Marcus' story as campaign for the 'Britain is GREAT' website and to further promote the Growth Vouchers project. This meant Marcus featured in videos, articles and billboards.

Not only was this great for Marcus (I love it when great things happen to great people, especially my clients), but it was great for me too. As a result of the case study, I got my first piece of national press and started to become widely known as a sales trainer and Growth Vouchers adviser. Not only that, but my name became well known across government departments such as the Department for Business, Innovation and Skill (BIS) now known as the Department for Business, Energy and Industrial Strategy (BEIS).

This had a ripple effect on my own business. Way back when I first found out about Growth Vouchers, I came across an article about a lady called Emma Jones. There was a photo of her in *The Sunday Times* standing outside 10 Downing Street. Emma is the founder of Enterprise Nation and is small business representative for the Crown. I could see that Emma was a force to be reckoned with and instantly knew I wanted her to be my friend. Imagine my surprise when several months later, Emma called me to speak at an event for her at Somerset House. I was asked to speak to other Growth Vouchers advisers about how they can promote the project. I was an adviser to the advisers.

To further promote the project, I collaborated with local business support organisations to host four roadshows, where businesses from each sector could explain how small businesses could use the vouchers to access their services. This not only raised awareness of the project, but of my brand. It gave me another opportunity to speak in front of my target audience about what I did, and as a result my client database began to grow.

Following all this excitement, I decided to apply for Small Business Saturday's Small Biz 100. Being chosen for this resulted in me running a Christmas market outside 10 Downing Street, where I met the Chancellor of the Exchequer and Baroness Brady. I think I am one of the few people who can say they have a photo outside Number

10 with their company roller banner. Not only that, but we made the national press. It wasn't that long ago I had seen Emma Jones outside Number 10 in *The Sunday Times* and wanted the same thing, and now I had done it.

Enterprise Nation decided to put on a competition that would result in a list of the UK's top 50 business advisers. Yes, my name was on the list, but not only was I in the top 50, I was made one of the UK's top 10 business advisers. All stemming from the work I had done alongside the Growth Vouchers project. In my book, once it's been said it can't be taken back, I now always refer to myself as one of the UK's top 10 business advisers.

The year 2014 had been a bit of a roller-coaster ride, but little did I know that the very best was still to come. Almost a year and a half later, I was invited to the Queen's Royal Garden Party for my dedication to Enterprise. I got to visit Buckingham Palace. BUCKINGHAM PALACE! When I first heard about the Growth Vouchers I knew I was onto something good, but I would never have imagined that it would lead me down a road to having afternoon tea with the Queen. To this day, I still don't know who put my name forward, but I have a strong inclination it was someone from BEIS. Sometimes it's not what you know but who you know. Oh, and if I didn't make it clear enough, visiting Buckingham Palace for the Queen's Royal Garden Party is one of the proudest moments of my career.

The next thing I ticked off my list was to win a national award. In November 2015, I won GB Entrepreneur of the Year Special Merit for Service. I was shortlisted at GBEA (Great British Entrepreneur Awards) a year previously but never won, but I didn't let that hold me back. Some of the GBEA winners have gone on to become household names, and this award was another step on the way to my destination. Perseverance paid off – if at first you don't succeed, try, try, and try again. I love GBEA for two reasons, one because I won (obviously) and two because it's a great platform for networking. I have three high profile clients, all young entrepreneurs who have managed to build businesses that turn over millions, and I met all three of them at the GBEA ceremony. If you want to be associated with the movers and shakers you have to hang out where they are.

I'd started to make a bit of a name for myself and had been working closely with Enterprise Nation as a Regional Champion. Not only did Emma Jones help me to become a feature on Radio 4, but she gave me the golden keys. In January 2016 I was asked to put together a group of 20 small businesses and take them to 10 Downing Street to speak to the prime minister's adviser about the future of the small business economy in the UK. I had gone past my original goal of standing outside Number 10, I was leading a trip and giving other small businesses the opportunity I had had. In two years, I had gone from the person wishing to get a photo of myself outside Number 10 to the person with the ability and authority to take other hopefuls and help them achieve their goals. I was becoming the mover and shaker, a person of influence.

The latest stop on the way to my destination has been the rebranding of my company, Sales Coaching Solutions, and turning it into the personal brand by which you know me today, Alison Edgar, The Entrepreneur's Godmother. I rebranded in May 2016, and, as with the Growth Vouchers, it has been a bit of a whirlwind ride. The connections I made over the past few years have made it easy for my new brand to catch on; when people see pink they know I'm in the room. The unique name elevated my brand awareness, enabling me to grow my product offering and expand my online following. I have been invited to speak at some amazing events, from a first-ever event of its kind in the Middle East to sharing the line-up with Lord Sugar and Mary Portas at QuickBooks Connect in London. Sometimes change can be scary, but it often leads to amazing things.

Awards are a great way to get PR and build awareness around your brand. In 2017 I was chosen as Mentor of the Year at the Bristol and Bath Women of the Year awards. Regional awards don't quite have the reach of nationals like GBEA, but that doesn't mean they can't open doors. When a journalist was looking to interview local business owners on their views surrounding the upcoming general election, they called me – and how did they find me? Well, my name came up after I won at the Bristol and Bath awards. As a result, I was interviewed for BBC Breakfast, not once or twice, but three times. For three consecutive weeks, I was featured on BBC Breakfast. It may have only been a regional award but it got me national TV, and even I didn't expect that level of coverage.

The last stop on my journey so far that I want to talk about is another experience of role reversal. I was asked to judge the Institute of Sales Management BESMA's (British Excellence Sales and Marketing Awards). I have made the shift from entering and trying to prove myself, to being recognised as an expert in my field and qualified to sit on the other side of the fence. As much as I love winning awards, I have always wanted to play Simon Cowell and judge, as I have always viewed the judges as being at the top of the chain, the experts, the influencers. And now I'm one of them.

The Vehicle

You know my strategy and the route I took to get there, but I want to go back and talk about what I call the 'vehicle' – the idea I had from the beginning that was the motivation behind starting my business and becoming The Entrepreneur's Godmother.

Most businesses have competition, they are not the only ones in the world who do what they do, so to make yourself different you need to create a unique brand which is different from your competitor's. If I told you my brand strategy is based on chocolate, you probably wouldn't believe me, but it's true, it is. My thought was there are loads of sales trainers and coaches in the world and even more business consultants that claim to be sales experts. If you have the choice of Cadbury Dairy Milk or a no-name chocolate bar, which one would you choose? Let's be honest, most of us would choose the Dairy Milk. So, I set out to be the Dairy Milk of the sales training industry.

It is fundamental to stand out from the crowd and be the best in class. You want to be known by as many people as possible for all the right reasons, your brand should be memorable for quality, have a slogan that people remember and a branding logo and colour that people recognise straight away, and like chocolate, the lasting taste of enjoyment that you will want more of and will tell your friends about.

Let me explain how my brand strategy was formulated around a bar of chocolate.

	Cadbury Dairy Milk	The Entrepreneur's Godmother
Quality	Consistent taste	Consistent sales message
Reputation	Award-winning	Award-winning
Slogan	A glass and a half of milk in every bar	When delivered correctly, sales and customer service are exactly the same thing
Colour	Purple	Pink
Logo	Glass of milk	The tiara
Recognition	High awareness in field	High awareness in field
Alignment	Stocked in well-known stores	Works with high profile organisations

As you will see from the table, one of the ways Cadbury Dairy Milk has become a best-selling, award-winning chocolate bar is by building a premium brand, having a top-quality product and having worldwide recognition. Without quality it would have been a flash in the pan as consumers would not continue to buy, and without bold branding it would not have stood out on the shelf and chocolate eaters would not have bought it. Hopefully, you can see why a strong marketing strategy is the foundation of my sales strategy.

Quality

I honestly don't think many people start their day planning to be mediocre. Most of us want to be the best we can, and certainly in sales if you want to be successful, being average should not be an option. But look at the start of this book where I talked about the 250 salespeople in the Madejski Stadium. The percentage of STARS was low, but how do you recognise who they are? For them it is apparent when their names, figures and longevity are called out. For me to prove quality, I became a member of a chartered institute in my field, which then proved to people who were looking for my services that I had gone through the effort of proving the quality of my services. Another step I took to prove the quality of my business was moving from a sole trader to an incorporated company and becoming VAT registered. That then gave me credibility to deal with larger organisations who insist on certain criteria.

What can you do to prove the quality of your product or service? If like me you're a service, you can become accredited by joining a professional body. If you provide a product, you could look at becoming ISO standard approved or register for a kite mark. As for selling the benefits, proving a certain level of quality is a great way to help overcome objections if someone is not sure.

Quality also leads to consistency. Every time I have eaten a Cadbury Dairy Milk bar the flavour and texture is the same, unless someone has left it in the sun of course, and that's not the fault of the manufacturer!

Reputation

It is never what you say about yourself, it's what others say about you that counts. A simple way to do this is by getting testimonials for the work you have done or what your customers say about you. No one likes to make a mistake when they buy, and the Greens and Blues especially need reassurance they are doing the right thing. Therefore, having testimonials will help to close more sales.

When I first started, I had never been a sales trainer before, and I had to get testimonials on LinkedIn from my peers who I had worked with to say how good I was at sales and I used this to close my first client. Then I asked them for a testimonial about the positive results they had seen from the work I'd done with them. They were happy to give me a testimonial, and soon I had enough client testimonials to start creating case studies. This helped to showcase my work further and prove the quality of my training. My reputation began to build and demand started to increase, which in business is what you ultimately want.

Recognition

Reputation and recognition are closely linked, and when your reputation grows so does your recognition. Winning awards elevates your profile, and not only is it an amazing feeling but it gives additional press and media coverage which leads to brand awareness. It's a bit like building a snowman – the more awards you win, the more recognition you get, the more your reputation grows and so on until you have gone from a few snowflakes to filling the front garden with a full-blown snowman complete with carrot nose and coal buttons.

My plan was always for national and international recognition. Throughout this book, and especially when I spoke about my route, you have read about some of the awards and accolades I have earned. I hope that from this you can generate some ideas about how you can elevate yourself and your business to become the leader in your field.

This is when it becomes more important than ever that you maintain a high level of quality. Bad reviews are like a hot day in winter, it won't take long for your fantastic snowman to melt, and you will have to start building it from scratch all over again.

Slogan

From some of the dates I refer to in the personal section, you will know that I'm more of a baby boomer than a millennial. The Cadbury Dairy Milk slogan from my era which I remember most and can still quote is: "A glass and a half of milk in every bar". The era of the slogan coincided with free school meals, when parents were encouraged to give their children more milk.

My slogan or mission statement is: "When it's delivered correctly sales and customer service are EXACTLY the same thing". I have it on my website, in my literature and I mention it all the time. It's a bit like a catchphrase, and I never tire of people quoting it to me.

Remember it's important to stand out from the crowd, and having a strong slogan is a great way to do just that.

Logo

Lots of companies are now letting the picture paint the words. On the new Dairy Milk bars the slogan has been dropped and the picture of a glass and a half stands alone because the brand awareness is so high. After I called myself The Entrepreneur's Godmother, I started to use a tiara as my logo – after all, every fairy godmother has a wand and a tiara. Now when my team create promotional graphics for social media I don't always have to use my full logo, I simply use a pink tiara logo, which my following clearly identify with being mine.

Colour

Everyone has competition whether you are a small business or a salesperson fighting to get to the top of the league table, and colour is a great way to stand out. When in need of a chocolate fix at the petrol station pay desk, you know that your Cadbury Dairy Milk will be in its little purple wrapper standing out from all the other chocolate bars.

It was always my mission to stand out from the crowd. To be fair, this isn't something I have ever struggled with due to my larger than life personality and hearty laugh. I am an extrovert so I like to be remembered, which is why you will always find me wearing something in pink, whether it's a dress, coat or even just some jewellery. Occasionally I have a non-pink day, and when I do this it usually causes quite a stir and people ask me why I'm not in pink. This is almost as effective as wearing the pink, and it shows that people associate me with my brand colours.

I initially started wearing pink because I wanted to be remembered at networking events and I stood out a lot more in pink than everyone else who wore black. Some like it that I stand out and others don't, but remember you are not going to sell to everyone, so it's ok to be bold.

Alignment to Movers and Shakers

Alignment to movers and shakers is a key ingredient to sales strategy and something I referred to when I spoke about my own strategy. It has always been Cadbury Dairy Milk's strategy to be positioned in all major supermarkets, garages, convenience stores and anywhere else they sell fast moving consumable goods. I think we can say their strategy is working out quite well, but they didn't just appear in all these shops, they had to sell themselves in by associating with the movers and shakers.

This is a strategy I have used to grow my own business. The movers and shakers are the big names, the key influencers in your industry. The idea is that you align yourself with the movers and shakers, firstly, because it helps build brand awareness, and secondly because it brings you closer to your target market.

One of the movers and shakers in my industry is Emma Jones. 'Why?' you ask. Well, Emma is the Queen of Enterprise, hence her business Enterprise Nation. I knew that being associated with someone of

Emma's stature would prove I was an expert in my field and make me more accessible to my target market of startups, micros and owner-managed businesses.

To achieve this, I put in place what I call the 'befriending' strategy. If you have noticed I now refer to Emma Jones as Emma, that's because three years on she is a dear friend who to this day never ceases to amaze me. I often say to Emma, "I can't believe it, you started off as a sales strategy and now you're one of my friends." For those of you who are wondering, yes, Emma knows she was part of my sales strategy, and it just goes to show what an effective strategy it was.

The 'Befriending' Strategy

So how did I become friends with the Small Business Representative to the Crown? Before I give away all my best-kept secrets (I'm terrible at keeping secrets), I should tell you that in sales as in business, there is no quick win. When you start a business you're in it for the long game. Don't expect things to change overnight. The key to the 'befriending' strategy is to be where the movers and shakers are.

1. **Utilise Social Media**

    Follow the movers and shakers on social media. Trust me, if they are really the key influencers they will be posting things online all the time. Here you will learn more about them, maybe you'll find out you don't want to be associated with them after all, or maybe you'll find out you have common interests. The best thing about following them on social media is they will tell you where they are going to be and what type of events they attend. Once you know where they will be, you can be where they are. By this, I don't mean hang out at their favourite restaurant until they turn up. I mean, if they attend events for certain charities or organisations, try to attend.

2. **Connect**

Before meeting the movers and shakers, it's a good idea to connect with them on LinkedIn. I say LinkedIn because it's a professional network, and someone may not want to connect with you on Facebook if they use it for close family and friends. Twitter is great, but it moves so fast that they probably won't even notice you unless you tag them in your tweets on a regular basis, but this can be a bit risky and lead to you being blocked.

My first contact with Emma was over Twitter, as it was the only way I could speak to her directly. I kept retweeting her posts until she followed me and I was able to message her privately to start a proper conversation. As I said, this can be a bit risky, and to this day I'm not entirely sure how I didn't get blocked.

3. **Make an Impact**

When you meet, use the W-Introduction formula to make an impact. Remember, first impressions count. Sometimes the fourth w, what's in it for them, can be tough, because as movers and shakers they will be able to do a lot by themselves. My top tip is be specific. I would say something along the lines of, "I have a strong network across the South West, particularly across Bristol, and would love to spread the word about what you're doing." I was specific about the location where my connections are, not just saying, "I have a big network". If I said that, I would definitely get some funny looks as most movers and shakers have large networks of their own.

4. **Follow-Up**

I'm going to go into this in more depth later, but following up is the key to every sale. Very rarely does someone buy first time, and this includes when you're selling yourself. You have already connected with them on LinkedIn, so send them a message and make it personal by relating to something you discussed when you met face-to-face. This way they are more likely to remember who you are.

5. Give Back

If you want to be associated with the big boys (or gals) then you must give them your time, whether it is helping shout about them on social media, getting involved with their campaigns or volunteering for their events. When I met Emma, do you think I said, "Oh, I'd love to help" and then walked away? Of course I didn't. I became an Enterprise Nation member, I took to social media to promote them and now I am the Regional Champion for the South West.

Everyone knows there is no such thing as a free lunch. I have given lots of my time promoting Emma and Enterprise Nation, partly because I wanted to be associated with them, but also because I genuinely believe they offer small business owners and entrepreneurs an amazing service. I am proud to be a Regional Champion.

What did I get out of it? To start with a good friend and business confidant and the association with Enterprise Nation, including being one of the chosen suppliers listed on their website. But the main thing is a mutual respect. Emma and I respect each other and understand business, I use my big Scottish mouth to shout about Enterprise Nation, and in return Emma has provided me with some fantastic opportunities as I mentioned earlier.

Who are the movers and shakers in your industry? Have a think. It may seem impossible to be associated with them at first, but let me tell you, nothing is impossible. Have you never heard of the six degrees of separation!

The Fuel

To get you to your destination you need fuel – you will never get there on an empty tank. I like to think of marketing and PR as the fuel, as they are the things that build your brand awareness and help you become recognised.

Social Media

I have already spoken about social media quite a bit, but as we all know, social media is fast becoming the centre of everything we do. So why wouldn't we use it to build relationships and make sales?

The majority of social media platforms can help you generate leads if you put the time and effort in. The big mistake lots of businesses make is they fail to interact with their online following – they post something then just leave it. For social media to be effective, you need to engage users in conversation. If someone likes or comments on a post, then start a conversation with them, using your open questioning techniques to understand their needs. Of course, there are lots of paid advertising options for social media, of which the key purpose of some is to generate leads. But like any savvy business person, you should utilise all the free features before paying for anything.

Facebook

The number one rule when it comes to Facebook is to try and keep your business and personal life separate. When you first start a business, approaching your friends and family through Facebook is the easiest way to gain a following. But don't make the mistake I made – as my business has grown so has my following and more and more people I meet request to become my friends on Facebook. When I first started my business I didn't see the problem with this and accepted everyone. A couple of years later I had thousands of Facebook friends I didn't really know. It became really difficult to know what to post. My family complained that I only ever posted about business and never shared photos of my kids, but at the same time I wasn't sure if I wanted to share personal family moments with people I didn't really know. It all got a bit confusing and I had to find a way to disentangle my business from my personal life.

A Facebook group was the answer for me. I already had a Facebook page, which I could invite people to like and where I could post and share things, but I found engagement was extremely low. Facebook only shows you things on your main feed if it thinks you'll be interested, so if you don't interact with anything on my page then the algorithm thinks you're not that interested and won't show my posts on your news feeds. However, pages are still great as they act almost as a website that people can use to find out about your products and services. They are also great for displaying customer reviews.

Facebook groups seem to work better for me. I was able to move my business friends from my personal profile to the group. Now my profile is only close personal family and friends and the group is where I keep my network updated about my business. My Facebook group is called the Entrepreneurs Can Clan and provides me with a place to post about upcoming events. The thing I love most about it is that it is an engaged community, and for some reason my following prefers to communicate on the group rather than the page. The Entrepreneurs Can Clan is continuously growing, and we get new member requests every day.

What works best for you will depend on your business. I have always built a community; therefore a group works better for me. But if you're a window cleaner, then a page would probably be best.

Twitter

I am not a social media expert, but I've been around the block a couple of times and have picked up some great tips along the way. As I said before, Twitter moves at an incredibly fast rate and most of the time users probably won't see your tweet, especially if they follow hundreds of people, let alone thousands.

The key to getting noticed on Twitter is using hashtags, but the hard part is finding the right hashtag for you. Some of the generic hashtags like #motivationmonday are widely searched for, but they are also widely used, which means it's going to be hard to hit your target audience with such a generic hashtag. There are some great tools online which show you what hashtags people in your industry use and search for. My top tip is to keep it relevant to your business, but not so niche that no one will ever find it. Of course, you can start your own, and this is becoming an increasingly popular trend, although you will need a large online following for it to have any real impact. Also, use more than one hashtag; if you've created your own, you could use that, then two of three popular ones.

The purpose of any social media platform, including Twitter, is to provide valuable and engaging content. Yes, you can use social media to sell your products and services, but you have to give before you can take. Selling online is like selling face-to-face. If you shout in someone's face "BUY MY PRODUCT! BUY MY PRODUCT!", they won't want to buy. But if you build a trustworthy relationship and provide them with valuable content, they might just think about buying something from you over a competitor.

It's also worth noting that Twitter is as much a place to share news as it is a social networking platform. When you log in to Twitter, you will see when you click on the 'Moments' tab it is basically a run-through of the latest news. This makes Twitter the number one place to share your articles and blogs.

Instagram

As much as I adore taking selfies and posting them on Instagram, it is the platform that is least effective for me. But that doesn't mean to say it won't work for you. Instagram is an image-led social platform, therefore it works amazingly well for product-based businesses, if you can display what you do visually then you need to be on it. If you're service-based this maybe a little difficult, although I do find it an effective platform to showcase events and workshops.

An aspect of Instagram I love is Instagram Stories. Stories enables you to take images that disappear after 24 hours, and not only that but if you have and use Stories, it will keep your profile icon on a bar along the top of the app, which is great for brand recognition. The photos posted onto an Instagram feed are often polished to perfection, since the person has usually put lots of effort into taking and editing the photo. I think this is why I struggle sometimes with this platform. As you know I'm 0% Blue so I have no patience and very little attention to detail. I would much rather just take a photo and stick it online, which is why I love the Stories element, as it doesn't matter how good my photo is because it will disappear after 24 hours. If you're attending an event, Stories is a great way of giving your followers a behind-the-scenes experience.

LinkedIn Strategy

As you can probably tell by now, LinkedIn is key to my strategy. LinkedIn is also a great way to find leads, especially if you're a B2B in the service industry. But, if you're also looking to sell into large retailers and corporations, LinkedIn makes it easy to find out who works where and who's in charge of what. I have one client who manufactures lingerie for women of all shapes and sizes. My client wanted to sell into high-end retailers, such as John Lewis and Harvey Nichols. The people who choose what to stock are usually called buyers. Together we used the advanced search options on LinkedIn to find out who the lingerie buyers were for each store. She then sent them a message and started a conversation. After sending some of her designs she had managed to schedule meetings with multiple buyers. It may take time and persistence, but it really can work.

LinkedIn has enabled me to grow my network bigger and faster than I ever could have done offline. Most people think you have to pay and become a LinkedIn premium member to really benefit from

LinkedIn, but this is so not true. Since starting my business in 2011, I have always used LinkedIn, but if you had told me when I first started that by persistently following my LinkedIn strategy I would gain my biggest international contract to date, well, I would have fallen off my chair.

I have a rule. Every time someone views my profile on LinkedIn, I connect and send them a personal message saying, "Hi, I'm Alison Edgar, The Entrepreneur's Godmother, I see you have viewed my profile. Were you looking for something specific or just widening your network?" Sometimes no one will reply, but more often than not people are polite and will respond accordingly. This is something I have always done and it has enabled me to generate some great leads that otherwise would have passed me by.

In September 2016 I did the same thing that I do every day, I checked my LinkedIn and practised my strategy, messaging a woman to thank her for viewing my profile. She replied a couple of days later, telling me she viewed my profile because she was looking for speakers for her event in Kuwait. That's right, in KUWAIT! At this point I really did fall off my chair. I followed the sales process, asking open questions, and when I felt the time was right, I requested a Skype call. If you're trying to make a big sale, always take it off social media when you can, but be careful, as doing it too soon can come across as a bit strong. I had a Skype call and continued to follow my sales process. To cut a long story short, LinkedIn is partly responsible for me speaking at the first ever event of its kind in the Middle East. Not only that, but it's what kicked off international export in my business.

When used correctly social media can be an amazing tool for businesses. And, Kuwait was amazing! From that one event, I have built long-lasting relationships and plan to visit again soon.

Public Relations (PR)

As you now know, my sales strategy incorporates a lot of PR. I am regularly featured in the press whether it's local magazines or national newspapers, like *The Sunday Times, The Telegraph* and *The Guardian*. I have also been featured on BBC Breakfast and the radio.

PR has two major benefits: one, it helps you to reach a wider audience as thousands upon thousands of people read magazines and newspapers every day. If you can be a feature in national or even local press, then it will help you to build your brand awareness and reach a wider audience. The second benefit of PR is the perception that comes with it. When someone sees you in a magazine, on TV or hears you on the radio, they assume that you are the expert, and it gives you that edge over your competitors. Using myself as an example, if you have the choice of two sales trainers, Joe Bloggs from down the road, or me, one of the UK's top 10 business advisers who you saw talking on the TV the other day. Who would you pick?

My top tip is to get to know the journalists and build a relationship. Sell yourself to them and getting media coverage will become a lot easier. Use the befriending strategy to meet them. This is easier with local journalists as they will hang out at local events. It's a little harder when it comes to the nationals, but it is doable. Here is an extreme real-life example of how I met the journalists for *The Mail on Sunday* and other national online publications. My good friends at Enterprise Nation organise Global Missions which enable businesses to visit potential new markets and conduct research. They were doing a mission to New York and I wasn't particularly interested in going, but then I saw that some of the big national journalists were going, so I booked a ticket, so that on the flight to New York I could network with the journalists. Like I said, this is an extreme case, although it did work, so just keep in mind that if you really want something there are ways of achieving it.

Acceleration

The fuel keeps you chugging along, but you will only move forward if you accelerate. Using marketing and PR to generate brand awareness is great, but ultimately you need more than brand awareness, you need sales, and the only way your business will ever grow is by earning cold hard cash. You need to sell your products and services. These are the true, pure, sales strategies I use to find clients and sell my products and services.

Networking Strategy

In the first couple of years of running my business every sale came from someone I had met when I was networking. I struggled to get marketing to work and, being honest, still do, that's why I'm a sales expect not a marketing expert. Without marketing the only way grow to my business was for me and my team to go out networking and make every sale ourselves. To this day, this is still responsible for a high percentage of our sales.

Some love networking and some absolutely hate it. But like anything in life, once you know how to do it, it isn't that hard. The key thing to remember is that everyone is in it for themselves. Do you remember when I gave you the example about the Titanic? Networking is the Titanic, and that's why it's really important you use the W-Introduction formula.

The strategy I use is marry, avoid, snog. It's essentially the same rules as snog, marry, avoid, but a little mixed up and all hypothetical of course. Before you start going around kissing anyone, I will tell you what I mean by this:

- **Marry** – These are the people who fit your ideal customer. The ones that need your product or service and are most likely to buy from you. Or they could be the movers and shakers, the people you want to associate with. Whether they're your ideal customer or key influencer, they are the ones you need to build long-term relationships with, the ones you want to marry.

- **Avoid** – These are the people that have nothing to offer, they don't fit your target market and will never spend money with you. There is no point spending your precious time with someone who is of no benefit to you. However, it has been known that even people you avoid may have connections you want to know, so don't write them off completely.

- **Snog** – These are the ones that you don't really know too much about, and no matter how much research you do, you struggle to find out anything about them. This means you will have to tal to them in person to find out if they could potentially be someone you want to marry. Sometimes you have to kiss a few frogs before you find your prince or princess.

How do you know who you want to marry, avoid and snog? Well, that's easy, do your research. The sales process begins before you even go networking. Event organisers will often send out a list of everyone attending a day or so before. This is when you should be using LinkedIn and their websites to conduct research and categorise everyone in marry, avoid and snog lists.

The secrets in the follow-up

Did you know that 44% of salespeople give up after one follow-up, yet 80% of sales require at least five follow-ups (HubSpot, 2017)? Following up is the key to sales, it's the not-so-big secret that everyone knows, yet no one follows up.

Even when you follow the networking strategy it is very rare that you will close the sale there and then. You can, but sometimes people (especially the Greens and Blues) will need more time to think about purchasing. The key to taking the lead and turning them into a paying customer is following up.

It can take between 5 and 12 touchpoints before someone buys. By touchpoints I mean points of contact, so this could be face-to-face, online, over the phone or even via direct mail. If you follow the strategies I have given in this book, then you should have had 3-4 touchpoints within the first day:

1. Connect on LinkedIn

2. Meet face-to-face

3. Follow up with email

4. Follow on Facebook and Twitter

After this, you need to continue building that relationship. People think you can only follow-up once, which is not the case. If someone is genuinely interested in purchasing something from you, they will view your persistence as a customer service. Remember my story about Newbury Racecourse, the man phoned me 12 times, but I didn't find it annoying, I thought it was a good customer service. He knew that I wanted to book tickets, and if he didn't follow-up and remind me and I forgot to buy the tickets, my whole family would have been upset.

The important thing when following up is to be sure that the person you're phoning really does have the potential to become a customer. The way you do this is by following the sales process, and if you've followed up several times and they still haven't bought, use the test intention technique.

No one is ever begging to hand over their cash. If you don't follow up they will get lost in your pipeline and you will have missed out on a sale.

Cold Calling

It's not 1984, we no longer need to make cold calls, and we have technology to help us. Picking up the phone is always the best way to contact someone, second to face-to-face that is.

In my opinion, cold calling is dead, and let's face it, most people don't like cold calls anyway. They come off as pushy and are often inconvenient. In case you've been living off the grid and don't know what I'm talking about… a cold call is a phone call from a company or business you don't know who are trying to sell you something. It's one of the easiest things to get wrong for anyone working in sales. But it's also not that hard to do it well…if you know how!

Some people, especially salespeople, will have no choice but to make cold calls, as it's a part of their job. Or maybe they're in an industry where cold calling is standard practice. Just because I think there are better ways to conduct business doesn't mean everyone else does.

I'm going to share some of my secrets for turning that cold call into a warm call.

Before I do that I want to share a cold calling experience I had which was one of the worst cold calls I have ever received. For the sake of the story, I'm going to name the caller Laura. Laura phoned my office to sell me web design services. I wasn't really interested but said she could email me with some details. I then replied to her email to say that after reviewing I wasn't interested in the service. She phoned again a week later and this is when things got ugly. When someone cold calls me, I start the timer to see how long it takes them to stop talking about themselves and actually ask me a question. Laura spent the first four minutes talking about herself, and it was clear she knew nothing about me or my business. When I objected again and said I had no need for her services, she replied, "That's fine, we also have a rebranding service that you might find useful as your logo and branding seem a bit dated." This is when I became a bad-day Red.

Firstly, what Laura failed to recognise was that my website had been rebranded two weeks prior to her call, so obviously I was a bit taken aback by her comment. Secondly, even if it had not been rebranded, what she said would still have been insulting and is no way to conduct a sales call. I won't drag out the details, but I can tell you it was the last time Laura called.

What can we learn from Laura's mistakes? Making a cold call is like making any other sale and therefore you should follow the process.

Here are my top tips for picking up the phone:

1. Make it warm

My first tip is to take that cold call and make it warm. The first step in the process is to do your research and that's exactly what you should do. If you can connect on LinkedIn and send a message, you should, then when you call you won't feel like a stranger to them. It's this which takes it from being cold to warm.

2. Engage the listener

Just like when you're networking, you need to engage the listener, which is why you use that W-Introduction formula. This is harder over the phone as someone can just slam the receiver down and cut you off, so you need to be quick. Jump in with the open questions early to engage them and build rapport.

3. Sell the benefits

Laura made the mistake of reeling off product features. Remember to always sell the benefits, but to do this you need to understand the customer's needs, which is why you need to engage them with open questions. It's all about process, my friends, it's all about process.

4. Be Polite

Being polite has never hurt anyone and it will certainly go down well with the person on the other end of the phone. Something I always do is say, "Are you okay to speak for a couple of minutes?" This is much more effective than jumping straight into the sale. We've all called people at inconvenient times, and if the person doesn't have time to speak they will only cut you off anyway, so it's best to ask first before delving into the details.

5. Follow-Up

Laura was right to follow-up, she just did it the wrong way. If you're going to follow-up, it's a good idea to schedule it with the customer on the original call, or request their email address and follow-up via email. That way they will be expecting it and won't be taken by surprise, and if they refuse to schedule another call, it's clear they're not interested and you can move on.

They key thing to take from this is, always do your research and follow the sales process. Had Laura done this, she would have understood more about me and my business, and engaged me from the beginning. If she had used open questions, she would have realised I had already had my website rebranded and identified on the original call that I wasn't in need of her services. These types of calls should be used to qualify leads. You shouldn't be trying to close at this point.

Cold calling, or warm calling as you should be doing from now on, doesn't have to be a negative experience. If you follow my 5 simple rules, both you and the potential customer can have a positive experience which could lead to a win-win situation.

Bingo Matrix

While the strategies above are about generating completely new leads, this strategy helps you get the most out of every customer relationship.

It's called the bingo matrix and the aim of the game is to get a full house. One of the best ways to increase sales is to sell to your original customers. Have you fulfilled all their needs or is there more you can do together? Hopefully you already have a strong relationship with them which makes it easier to upsell, as they trust you. I want to make it clear that even when upselling, you should only be providing products and services that meet the customer's needs. Trying to flog them everything you can will destroy the bond and trust you have built.

As a sales trainer, I provide training and coaching to my clients in the hope that at the end of the programme they can spread their wings and fly. After all, if they needed me to train them forever I wouldn't be doing a very good job. But that doesn't mean I can't upsell. I always make a point of checking in on my existing clients. If they take on a new salesperson or find they are struggling to hit targets, this is when I can upsell my products and services. If you don't have a wide range of products or services, you could upsell volume, for example, negotiate a larger order, or you could provide maintenance services, as this is a great way to generate recurring income if you're product-based.

Below is a table that I use to help me maximise every customer relationship. Down the side are all the products and services I can provide and along the top are the names of my customers.

	Customer 1	Customer 2	Customer 3	Customer 4
Team Training	x			
1-1 Coaching		x		
Online sales course	x	x		
Guide to starting a business	n/a	x		
Sales workshop				
Public Speaking Masterclass				

You want to get a full house, so if you go along and see an empty box, this is your opportunity to upsell. You will also see I have put in 'n/a' because sometimes a customer won't have a use for a certain product or service, and you should only ever be selling the customer what they need.

This strategy, albeit a sales strategy, also provides your customers with a good service. It encourages you to phone them, build the relationship and see how you can work together further. A lot of the time your customers won't even be aware of the different products and services you offer, and by doing this exercise you potentially save them the time and effort of finding a new supplier. When delivered correctly, sales and customer service are exactly the same thing.

Traffic Jams

Like any well-planned journey, there are always things that hold us back, such as unexpected traffic jams. One of the biggest traffic jams that holds the majority of my customers back and sometimes even holds me back is a lack of time. So many business owners tell me that they don't have time for this and they don't have time for that.

When I train sales teams, I see salespeople who don't follow-up with prospects because they don't have time.

Obviously, there are only so many hours in a day and we can't do anything about that, but we can do something about the way we manage our time. The time management system I teach my clients is based on Dr Steven Covey's example of rocks in a jar. Covey's demonstration uses rocks, pebbles, sand and a jar to demonstrate how you can manage time, and if you haven't seen this already I recommend it. There are loads of videos online.

The system I teach is called 'Alison's Big Balls' which is both amusing and effective. First, you need to write a list of your tasks and categorise them based on whether they are urgent or important. We then split these into three lists:

- **Basketballs** – Tasks that are both urgent and important, these are the ones you need to complete first – after all, a basketball to the face hurts.

- **Tennis balls** – These are the tasks that are urgent but not important. You have to watch these, as if you're not careful they will become basketballs.

- **Ping pong balls** –These are important but not urgent. They are the things that would be nice to do but don't need to be done right now.

If you have a task that is neither urgent nor important, then remove it from your list, as it's just a blocker.

I use an online tool called Trello that enables me to easily create the three lists of basketballs, tennis balls and ping pong balls. You can then add each task and move it from one list to the other. I also like to create a 'Yay, it's done' list that you can move all completed tasks to – this can be quite satisfying! The great thing about Trello is that you can share your lists and boards with your team, so you can work together on projects and leave notes on each task. Of course there are other tools you can use. Trello is just the one that has always worked well for us.

As a business owner, it can be hard to keep up with all aspects of the business, and that's why I always use my big ball system to make time for sales.

The Destination

This is the last stop on your journey and what everything should have been building towards. I won't tell you my destination just yet – you'll have to wait until the end of the book for that.

When determining your destination, it's important to break it up into smaller goals as this will make it easier for you to reach your end goal. If you just set one big goal, you might find you get lost on the way. Setting smaller objectives helps keep you on track and also gives you something to celebrate along the way, as it's important to appreciate the small things.

When setting goals, I always use the SMART system:

S = **S**pecific

M = **M**easurable

A = **A**chievable

R = **R**elevant

T = **T**ime based

This is a great formula to follow as it makes you think about the practicality of the goal you're setting. If you've worked in the corporate world, you've probably set one or two of these. A mistake many people make is drawing up a list of SMART objectives and then hoping that they'll achieve them with no extra work. SMART is the basis of your goal, you are the one who ultimately has to put in the hard work to achieve it.

By now you should have realised why strategy is so important. I have shared my strategy journey with you, but it's up to you to work out your own destination, which route you're taking and which vehicle you're travelling in.

PILLAR FOUR

CONFIDENCE

Confidence is something that comes naturally to some and is a daily slog for others to achieve. As a Yellow/Red, I'm a natural extrovert, therefore meeting people and having all eyes on me is something I've always relished. But nobody is perfect and there are aspects of my life in which even I am not very confident!

I've always had a young team since starting my business, and in the early days I had two amazing girls working from me, the lovely Natasha and Gemma. Both were keen bloggers, and I would see them write their blogs and then read the comments they would get and think to myself, "I wish I could do that". I'm dyslexic, I didn't do particularly well at school and I have always struggled when it comes to reading and writing. After months of wishing and hoping I could blog, the girls encouraged me to start blogging. They believed I could do it and so I did it. I loved it, and I definitely had a case of blogging fever to begin with. Okay, so my blogs weren't perfect and they were littered with spelling and grammatical errors, but my readers didn't care, so why should I. Now look at me, or look at you, you're reading my book. It was blogging that gave me the confidence to write a book.

In the world of sales, a word I hear all too often is 'can't'. Just like how I would say, "I can't blog because of my spelling" people often tell me they can't sell. It wasn't true that I couldn't blog so it's not true when someone says they can't sell. When you know how, selling becomes a lot easier, and that's why when I teach my Four Key Pillars of Sales methodology I leave confidence to last, because when you understand behaviours, know the sales process and have a strategy, confidence starts to come naturally.

Supermodel of Sales

At this point when I teach my sales workshop, I show a photo of the model Kate Moss on the screen and ask the attendees, "Am I Kate Moss?" This is when I get some funny looks and people start looking at me as if I'm delusional. Then one of the extroverts in the room will call out, "I've never seen you both in the same room at the same time", and as much as this makes me laugh and I would love to be Kate Moss, I'm not. But that doesn't stop me from waking up every morning, looking in the mirror and seeing the supermodel of sales.

I am the supermodel of sales! When I look in the mirror, I don't see a woman in her 50s with bad skin, I see someone with a natural skill to teach others to sell, someone who inspires others to start and grow businesses. I know I'm good at what I do, and when I know it, so does everyone else.

My ethos in life is "I think I am, therefore I am". This means when you believe something it becomes true, a little bit like a self-fulfilling prophecy. When you have confidence in yourself, others have confidence in you. It's the same when you doubt yourself.

Impostor Syndrome

Most of the time when people lack confidence, it's because they don't feel good enough. I see it all the time: business owners who struggle to sell their product because they think someone else could make it better. Do you ever have that feeling that, no matter what you do, it will never be good enough?

Don't worry, it's very common to feel this way. In fact it even has a name. It's called impostor syndrome.

Impostor syndrome is a term often used to describe high-achieving individuals who have an inability to recognise their own accomplishments, as they are persistently fearful of being exposed as a 'fraud'. Even when the evidence clearly shows they have achieved success, they pass it off as being down to luck and not actually as a result of anything they have done.

Those who suffer from impostor syndrome experience feelings of self-doubt, fear and anxiety, and struggle to enjoy success, and as a result hold themselves back.

Does any of this sound familiar to you?

It's OK to feel like this, and I think we all do at some point in our lives. I will let you into a little secret – I suffered from impostor syndrome myself when I started my business. My husband would joke that I was just playing at it, and to be honest I was. With my upbringing, I thought only tradesmen and the 'well to do' had their own businesses. I was neither of these things. I've always been hardworking, but as an employee starting my own business had never even crossed my mind.

I knew I had a passion for sales and a natural ability to teach others. I knew what I wanted to do. I wanted to start my own business sharing my knowledge and experience of doing what I do best.

I knew I could sell. I had been a top performer for some of the UK's best-known companies, sometimes achieving 3000% over target. I had mentored other salespeople, but I'd never been a sales trainer, or run my own business. Deep down, I knew I could achieve anything I wanted to achieve, but what if someone caught me out. What if they could tell I wasn't a sales trainer? I feared that other people were probably better than me. I feared that I was an impostor!

I continued to "play at it" until one day I was at a networking event and one of my pals said, "Hey, Alison, that guy over there wants sales training, you should go talk to him". At first I said, "Noooo, he doesn't want me, he wants a real sales trainer". It was at this point I realised I *was* a real sales trainer and that the only person stopping me was me. I walked up to the guy and secured my first client and haven't looked back since.

I think I am, therefore I am. The only true way to overcome impostor syndrome is to believe in yourself. This isn't going to happen overnight. It takes a little while to build up self-belief and confidence, but there are a few things that helped me when I was suffering from impostor syndrome and felt like my business wasn't good enough and I would like to share them with you.

These are my top 10 tips for overcoming impostor syndrome:

1. Do your research

When I set up my business, one of the things holding me back was this niggling thought at the back of my mind that maybe nobody wanted sales training. I had spent 15 years selling advertising to small businesses and had witnessed first-hand that when the phone didn't ring, small businesses didn't know how to proactively sell.

Yet I still doubted myself. I needed concrete evidence that what I knew wasn't just an idea. I did a survey. I approached all my old clients to find out more about their sales and to check if what I had thought all along was true. It turns out it was – small businesses were struggling to sell because they didn't know how to.

If you are running a business and doubt your idea, then do some research. Likewise, if you are a salesperson for someone else, if you doubt what you're selling, then do some research to put your mind at ease.

2. Unique Selling Point

Impostor syndrome makes you doubt yourself as you are constantly comparing yourself to others. Why would someone want sales training from me when they could get it from an experienced training provider? To overcome this I looked at what made me different, what I had that made me valuable to others, what my unique selling point was. I realised that my experience in hospitality management and sales was what gave me an advantage over some other sales trainers.

This helped me come up with my vision, "When delivered correctly, sales and customer service are exactly the same thing", which led to a new approach to sales training that my competitors weren't doing.

Nobody is the same, and we all have something to offer, whether it's a unique feature on your product or special skills you have as a business owner or salesperson. Find out what makes you different and embrace it.

3. Check out the competition

This is one of the most important steps towards self-belief, because comparing yourself to your competition only holds you back.

Everyone has competition. Look at Coca-Cola. They are the market leader, but did that stop Pepsi? No, of course it didn't. Competition is a good sign, as it means there is a market for what you do, that there's a demand for what you can provide. If you have figured out what makes you different, this will give you the upper hand when selling to potential customers.

As odd as it may seem, competition is good for business, it keeps everyone on their toes and can sometimes lead to collaborative strategic partnerships.

4. The price is right

Putting a price on something is tough, and this was something I found particularly tricky. Service industry costing is a bit like buying a house – it's worth what someone is prepared to pay for it. When you deliver a service, someone is essentially paying for your time, skills and knowledge. If you don't value what you can offer then you will undercharge. Pricing a product is a little easier as you can calculate margins and know exactly how much it cost to produce. At the same time, it can be difficult to put a value on something you are very passionate about.

When setting the price for my service, I decided to reach out to my competitors and look at what they were charging. I found out I was undercharging and felt more comfortable about increasing my price.

If you're feeling anxious about charging more for your product or service, ask yourself "What value am I delivering to my customers?" I know that sales are the lifeblood of any business and if you can't sell you don't have a business.

And remember, you can always negotiate down, but never up.

5. Don't wait for perfection

You need to be happy with your product or service before you can sell it, but if you wait for perfection you'll be waiting forever.

It's easy to find excuses why you're not ready to start selling. For instance, I wanted a case study for my website. That was my crutch, the thing that held me back. Until I had it, I didn't feel I could sell my services. I soon got over this after working with my first client.

6. Build a strong network

Becoming a business owner can be lonely. It comes with extreme highs, but also difficult lows. I'd be lying if I told you it never crossed my mind to jack it all in and get a "proper job".

From day one I had a business coach to help keep me on track. She listened to me and helped me remember the reasons I started the company in the first place, and why small businesses need my help to survive. It would have been downright rude of me to leave them in their time of need!

Why do your customers need you? Always remember this, and it will see you through your darkest hour.

I also have a strong group of business friends I frequently spend time with, chatting and laughing. Happiness is contagious, and it's a true fact that **"happy people sell"**.

7. Recruit the right people

Surrounding yourself with the wrong people makes you doubt yourself and makes you doubt the service you provide and your business as a whole, which affects your confidence when it comes to selling.

8. Get off the hamster wheel!

Sometimes we get so engrossed in running the business that we forget to work on it. Take a step back and look at what the future holds for your company. I see so many business owners spending all their time doing the short-term work that pays the money. Very rarely do they take time to look at the long-term vision. If you only ever look at the here and now, you will struggle to progress and identify avenues for growth.

9. Believe in the power of your customers

Testimonials are a very powerful way to reassure potential customers that you're a good choice. When you struggle to have confidence in yourself, reading your customer reviews will give you the boost you need.

Make sure you read and digest their positive feedback. They are saying wonderful things about YOU, not someone else. You are not an impostor in their eyes. You are the white knight who has entered their world to solve their problem.

10. Set Goals

Goals are ultra-important in business. They are the things which drive you on to overcome your fears. Without them you will flounder, and lose focus. Without focus you will doubt yourself, and feel that other people are better than you. **The more goals you achieve, the more confidence you will gain.** You'll soon start to believe that you are not an impostor, you are the "real deal".

If you follow my tips, you'll find yourself doing things differently. **You'll overcome impostor syndrome.** If you dig deep you will find the confidence you need to believe in yourself and your product or service.

A Case of Confidence

Do you remember in strategy when I told you about Growth Vouchers and how I would run roadshows to promote them? At one of the roadshows I met a lovely lady in her 50s, Carol Aplin. At the age of 57, Carol had made the brave decision to start her own business, Pink&Green Skincare. She had a background as a holistic and skincare expert and had used her knowledge to develop a range of organic and natural skincare products to empower women.

Like everyone else, Carol attended the roadshow to gain new business skills. After hearing all the speakers, she decided her biggest problem was that she couldn't sell and that I was the person who could help her.

Talking to Carol, the first thing I noticed was that she was a Green, quiet, shy and reserved. Pretty much everything I'm not. I could tell Carol knew exactly what she was talking about when it came to skincare and she had a real passion. She had an entrepreneurial spirit that was fighting to make her business a success. The second most poignant thing I understood about Carol was that her problem wasn't she couldn't sell – she didn't have the confidence to sell because, of course, she hadn't been shown how. As I have already told you, there's no such thing as 'can't', and if you're willing to learn like Carol was then you will soon realise that for yourself.

In our first session, I had already decided it was my mission to turn the quiet, shy lady I had met at the roadshow into a confident and compelling businesswoman. Like a lot of us, Carol started her business because she saw a gap in the market. She knew there was a demand for natural and organic skincare products, but she just didn't think people would want to buy them from her. She was suffering from impostor syndrome, as she couldn't understand why anyone would want to buy beauty products from a 57-year-old. To this my response was "Why wouldn't they?"

Over a number of sessions I worked with Carol, teaching her the Four Key Pillars of Sales. The behaviours helped her to understand why she was who she was, and we took the sales process and made it fit for her business and together worked on long- and short-term strategies. Once Carol knew how to sell it became a lot easier.

Before working together, Carol was the one to hide at the back of the room. Now when I see her at networking events she works the room and can deliver her W-Introduction with pure confidence. Not only was there an increase in Carol's confidence, but her newly learned sales skills led to a 150% increase in sales and a 400% increase in leads. It just goes to show that sometimes it really is just a case of confidence, or a lack of it, holding you back.

I wanted to tell you this story because I think the change I have witnessed in Carol is quite possibly the biggest transformation I have ever seen. Self-doubt and a lack of confidence is something we all suffer from at some point in our lives and can really hold us back from doing the things that make our hearts sing. If you think you can't do something, sit down and ask yourself why, and you'll probably find it's your confidence holding you back because there's no such thing as 'can't'.

One person in my life who is a great example of natural confidence is my Mum's sister, my Aunt June. I remember when Aunt June came to visit and we were doing our usual thing of relaxing in the hot tub and having a family BBQ. When the temperature started to dip, I lent Aunt June my jacket. It was a baby pink blazer and far too big for her. She put it on and I said, "Ooh, Aunty June, you look good in that." She turned and said, "Of course I do, hen, I look great in everything." If Aunt June can have this unfaltering confidence at the age of 80 after all she's been through, we sure as hell can too.

Glasgow to Cape Town

In the late 80s and early 90s, I travelled the world for six years, working in international hotel management.

As a 20-year-old, single female, who had only ever ventured outside of the UK on a package holiday to Spain, the thought of leaving my friends, family and everything I knew in Scotland to explore the big wide world was a mostly exciting but also daunting prospect. As much as I was excited to be the one leaving home and setting out on an adventure, I was full of fear.

On 26th November 1998, the day before my 21st birthday, something happened to me which changed my life forever. The most poignant thing about my tale is that the person who had such an impact on me does not know to this day who I am and what effect he has had on my life.

Prior to the electronic scanners at airport departures, there used to be a human being who checked your boarding pass before you entered security. They would ask your destination to make sure it matched your ticket. When the tear-stained face of Alison McColl (my maiden name) arrived at the departure point at Glasgow Airport, the guard duly asked, "Where are you going, hen?". I managed to sob to him that I was leaving all my friends and family in Glasgow to go and live in Cape Town. It was his one-sentence reply that, unbeknown to him, helped shape me into the woman I am today. He said, "Well, hen, I'll tell you what… it's Cape Town's gain and Glasgow's loss!"

It is with this sentiment I live my life and have built my sales career and company. When the man said that to me, it confirmed everything I already knew, that I had made the right decision to leave home and move to Cape Town. It taught me to value my gut instinct and trust my own decision, and it gave me confidence. It was this that made me realise that you can't please all the people all the time, but you have to have confidence in the decision.

Sales is a numbers game: the more people you talk to, the more people will want to buy you or your product. Are you going to sell to everyone? It would be nice, but of course you're not. You have to be resilient – there will always be people that no matter how you overcome their objections or negotiate, you will not be able to influence. Don't get upset or frustrated, move on, their loss is the next person's gain.

Win-Win Mindset

At the beginning of this book, I spoke about fixed and growth mindset and the importance of this as an entrepreneur and salesperson. A growth mindset is essential. Being able to accept change and learn new things is the only way your business will be a success.

Another area of mindset is a win-win mindset. Now I'm not a psychologist so everything that I share with you is from my own experience and observation. We know that sales is a numbers games and you will never sell to everyone, even Apple hasn't managed that. You have to believe in yourself, because no one else is going to do it for you. Do you think that when Usain Bolt steps up to the starting line he thinks, "I don't think I'll bother today, I'll just come second"? Like hell he does. He has the heart and mind of a winner, he goes into every race believing he can win. He gives 110% every time. This is the same with sales – you need to have the mind of a winner. You should enter every sale, every negotiation, every client meeting knowing that you have what it takes to close the deal.

MY SECRETS

What are the Secrets of Successful Sales?

Hopefully, as you have worked your way through this book, you have now got a clear understanding of how to sell, but here is a little recap:

1. You have to want to sell, and if you continually tell yourself you can't, you will not be able to. Use Growth Mindset to believe everything is possible and achievable. After all, up until recently I never thought I could write a blog let alone a book, and now look at me, a published author.

2. Aim for the STARS, effort equals reward. There is an old saying, "The more I dial the luckier, I get". Statistically, the more people you speak to, the more you will sell to. Remember to follow my methodology and don't sell too soon. Managing your time wisely and focusing on sales activity will help you get "luckier"!

3. Know the difference between Sales and Marketing. Unless you trade 100% online, it's always sales that will put the ball in the hole. Becoming a Cadbury Dairy Milk bar will help you sink the putt more often.

4. Understand your behaviours and that of your customers, adapting is key. Remember to treat other people how they want to be treated, not how you want to be treated.

5. Know the process. Ultimately people buy people, and by following the process you will have more structure and it will help you build a stronger relationship which will mean you will sell to more.

6. Have a strategy! You need a destination, because without it you are never going to get there. I promised you earlier I

would share mine… I want to be the Adele of Sales Training. Adele has an amazing talent which she has perfected, and when she sings she touches the souls of people around the world. This book is my equivalent of her first album *19*. It's not been written in a quest for fame and fortune, but I know what I teach works, and by following my methodology it will change the destiny of my readers around the world.

7. Have confidence in yourself. You need to believe you are the "Supermodel" of what you do. If you do not have confidence in yourself, other people will not have confidence in you. Dig deep and find the heart of a winner.

8. Learn to love sales. Like me as a novice golfer, you can either whinge and moan about it, or you can take my techniques and practice, practice, practice until you love it.

9. Always remember my motto: "When it's delivered correctly, sales and customer service are exactly the same thing". This will help you to sell from the heart and realise that by not asking for the order you are doing the customers a disservice.

10. You will not sell to everyone, but stay positive and remember it's "Glasgow's loss and Cape Town's gain" and when you get one 'no', it's a step closer to a 'yes'.

I would like to thank you for buying this book and moving me one step closer to being Adele.

Happy Selling

REFERENCES

Dweck, C. (2006). *Mindset: The New Psychology of Success*. New York. Random House. Pages 7-9.

HubSpot. (2017). *107 Mind-Blowing Statistics That Will Help You Sell Smarter*. [Online] Available at: https://blog.hubspot.com/sales/sales-statistics [Accessed 19th September 2017]

Morgan, C. (2016). *5 Little Known Facts About Body Language That You May Not Know*. **Huffington Post. [Online] Available at:** http://www.huffingtonpost.com/dr-carol-morgan/5-little-known-facts-about-body-language-that-you-may-not-know_b_8011004.html **[Accessed 23rd August 2017]**

Statista. (2017a). *Number of internet users worldwide from 2005 to 2017.* **[Online] Available at:** https://www.statista.com/statistics/273018/number-of-internet-users-worldwide/ **[Accessed 14th September 2017]**

Statista. (2017b). *Number of Social Media Users Worldwide from 2010 to 2021.* **[Online] Available at:** https://www.statista.com/statistics/278414/number-of-worldwide-social-network-users/ **[Accessed 14th September 2017]**

WORK WITH THE ENTREPRENEUR'S GODMOTHER

Enjoyed the book and want to work with me further? You can!

It doesn't matter what stage of business you're at or even if you don't have your own business and just want to excel as a salesperson, I can help you reach your goals and knock it out the park.

I understand that everyone learns differently that's why I have created a number of different options for you to work with me:

- Enrol on my online courses

- Attend a live workshop

- Work 1-2-1 through my coaching packages

- Take me on as your consultant

- Bring me in to train your team

For more information on how you can have me as your very own Entrepreneur's Godmother, head over to www.alisonedgar.com

WHAT OTHERS SAY ABOUT WORKING WITH THE ENTREPRENEUR'S GODMOTHER

"Alison is the queen of sales and one of the most well-connected women we have ever met, she helped us to expand into new markets and raise brand awareness, enabling us to elevate the business as we grow geographically."

Mark Wright, Founder of Climb Online, Winner of The Apprentice 2014 and Business Partner of Lord Alan Sugar and Raife Wieland, Regional Sales Manager at Climb Online

"Alison provided sales training and coaching to the team at GripIt Fixings, she's a pleasure to work with and has given the office staff a huge boost in their confidence levels."

Jordan Daykin, Founder of GripIt Fixings and youngest contestant to receive investment from Deborah Meaden on BBC's *Dragon's Den*.

"Alison Edgar is absolutely fantastic. I attended a training course run by Alison, and the following week used the skills learned in a client meeting, where I managed to secure our largest order ever! Her enthusiasm is contagious and she helps provide real results to individuals and businesses alike. We use Alison's e-learning course in our office and it helps us set goals and move the business forward. I regularly recommend Alison to my business contacts."

Simon Crowther, Founder of Flood Protection Solutions and multi-award winning entrepreneur, including GB Young Entrepreneur of the Year 2016.

"Alison's training has been incredible for my business. The training is great for any size business and especially when your team need to learn the fundamentals of sales! We found the personal behaviour profiles very useful and enabled me as a CEO to understand my team's strengths and weaknesses."

Julianne Ponan, Founder and CEO of Creative Nature and BBC's *Dragon's Den* Contestant.

JOIN MY COMMUNITY

Business can be a lonely place, so it's important to have a strong network surrounding you. I created my private Facebook group, Entrepreneurs Can Clan, to support entrepreneurs and share sales advice. The Clan is a secure environment where you can meet like-minded individuals, network and access business support.

Just search '**Entrepreneurs Can Clan**' on Facebook to join.

You can also keep up with me across other social media platforms:

Facebook Page: The Entrepreneur's Godmother

Twitter: @aliedgar13

Instagram: entrepreneurs_godmother

LinkedIn: Alison Edgar

I look forward to connecting with you online!

REGISTER YOUR BOOK

Join the club and register your book to receive exclusive content, discounts and more.

You'll be added to my mailing list and receive monthly updates and tips and you'll be the first to know about new products and workshops.

Simply scan the QR Code below or visit https://alisonedgar.com/book-registration/

WHEN DELIVERED CORRECTLY, SALES AND CUSTOMER SERVICE ARE EXACTLY THE SAME THING.

The
Entrepreneur's
Godmother®

Alison Edgar

ABOUT THE AUTHOR

Alison Edgar was born in Clydebank, Scotland, the same town which saw the birth of the QE2, Wet Wet Wet, and one of the UK's most famous entrepreneurs, Duncan Bannatyne.

As a dyslexic, school was always difficult, so at the age of 16, Alison's love of people led her to leave school and enter the world of hospitality; within a few years she managed hotels in Cape Town, Sydney, Ayers Rock and the Channel Islands. It was on her return to the UK that she found her calling for sales and became a top performer with some of the world's best-known blue chip companies.

This was where her love of entrepreneurship and small businesses began. On a daily basis for over 30 years she would be embroiled in what business people did, and how and why they did it that way. During this time she discovered many businesses didn't understand the difference between sales and marketing. They were heavily reliant on marketing to make the phone ring, but when it didn't, they did not know how to sell proactively and all too frequently went out of business. In characteristic fashion, she thought 'not on my watch' and decided to do something about it.

So Alison became 'The Entrepreneur's Godmother', giving entrepreneurs the skills they need to sell their fantastic products and services. Working with her, some of her clients have gone on to create multi-million-pound companies.

When she is not being 'The Godmother', she is mother to sons Kieran and Connor and wife to Neil, and enjoys seeing as much of the world as she can.

42487608R00087

Printed in Poland
by Amazon Fulfillment
Poland Sp. z o.o., Wrocław